RICK O'SHAY

BY STAN LYNDE

The Dailies: 1961-1962

Introduction by Stan Lynde

*Layouts, mechanicals, and production
by Lynda Brown Lynde*

OTTONWOOD
Publishing, Inc.

*2340 Trumble Creek Road
Kalispell, Montana 59901-6713*

1-800-937-6343

Rick O'Shay, The Dailies: 1961-1962

Cottonwood Graphics, Inc.,
2340 Trumble Creek Road,
Kalispell, MT 59901-6713
1-800-937-6343

LIBRARY OF CONGRESS
CATALOG CARD NUMBER 95-068475

ISBN 1-886370-01-X

Printed in U.S.A.

First Printing: 1 September 1995

135798642

INTRODUCTION

In 1962 I came home to Montana after living in and around New York City for the previous seven years. I don't recall kissing the ground upon arrival, although that's the way I felt--and feel--about the state. I do remember that I was delighted to have come home at last, and from that day forward Rick O'Shay was produced for a growing readership around the world from one of the smallest states in terms of population and one of the largest in terms of area.

A New York booster of bigness once asked me (facetiously) if we had anything to compare with Manhattan out in the wilds of Montana. There *is* a town in Montana named Manhattan; it has a population of just over 1,000 souls compared with the 8 million or so who inhabit its more famous eastern namesake. Anyway, I admitted we had no metropolis so grand in Big Sky country, but said I did know of several mountain canyons which could pretty much swallow up the entire Big Apple--skyscrapers, stock exchanges, muggers, and all.

At any rate, I came home to my roots, and so did Rick. I've regretted a number of my decisions over the years, but never that one. Producing the strip among the people who inspired it and in the places that provided its spirit gave it a quality I don't believe it would have had if done from another place. Even if that were not so, my return to Montana brought a sense of contentment and completeness to the strip's creator, at least.

1961 and 1962 saw the strip begin to hit its stride as I learned to write and draw it better. The characters, their personalities, and their relationships began to develop more fully, and the stories took some first steps toward a later pattern of alternating satire and comedy with action and adventure.

I was happy in my work then, and I think it shows. My hope is that you will enjoy this book, whether you're reading these stories for the first time or for the tenth. After all, it is you the reader who has made my long ride with Rick and company possible.

Much obliged.

Stan Lynde

The Unmentionables

Television was still in its infancy when *Rick O'Shay* began its syndicated life in the spring of 1958. All three major networks--NBC, CBS, and ABC--carried "westerns" on prime time to the near exclusion of other kinds of programming, and I found fertile ground for satire among the more cliche' ridden horse operas of the period.

By 1961, however, the climate had changed. By then, the networks had begun to turn away from tales of the West toward a near-saturation of private detective and police shows. *The Untouchables*, starring Robert Stack as the incorruptible Eliot Ness, was among the most popular of the breed, and--in my opinion--was among the best of the bunch.

The premise behind *Rick O'Shay* at the time was that the characters and locales portrayed in the strip existed somewhere in the present-day west. This concept provided great opportunities for satire--and culture shock--as the modern world broke in on the people of Conniption, and vice versa.

One of my favorite methods of creating stories for the strip was to pose the question "what if." When I asked myself "what if" an elite, straight-arrow force of crime fighters came to clean up the town of Conniption, *The Unmentionables* story was the result. East met west, the cap and ball revolver met the tommy gun, and before you could say "Hi Yo, Time Warp, Away" anachronism rode again!

WHY SO GLOOMY, CHIEF.. YOU GOT TROUBLES?

I'VE GOT TROUBLES THAT SHOULDN'T HAPPEN TO A PALEFACE, RICK..

1-23

MY GOLF GAME IS TERRIBLE, MY RHEUMATISM IS ACTIN' UP, AND I'VE MISLAID MY DENTURES..

..BUT WORST OF ALL, BUSINESS IS WONDERFUL! NEARLY ALL MY ENTERPRISES SHOW HUGE PROFITS!

WELL.. WHAT'S WRONG WITH THAT?

WHAT'S WRONG? I'LL HAVE TO SELL OUT COMPLETELY TO PAY MY TAXES!

STAN LYNDE

© 1961 by The Chicago Tribune.

1-24

YES, RICK.. IT'S NOT EASY.. BEING AN INDIAN.

ACCORDIN' T' HISTORY, IT NEVER WAS, CHIEF.

STAN LYNDE

EVERY DAY MORE PALEFACES COME HERE TO OUR RESERVATION.. FRANKLY, RICK.. MY PEOPLE ARE WORRIED.

HOW COME, CHIEF? THAT'S PROGRESS, AIN'T IT?

BEWARE THE PRAIRIE DOG

PERHAPS.. BUT LET A PALEFACE MOVE INTO A NEIGHBORHOOD AND PROPERTY VALUES ALWAYS GO DOWN!

© 1961 by The Chicago Tribune.

1-25

BUT ENOUGH OF MY TROUBLES, RICK.. SUPPOSE WE WATCH SOME TELEVISION?

SUITS ME CHIEF.. WHAT'S ON?

OH, THE USUAL.. MAYHEM AND MURDER.. DEATH AND DESTRUCTION.. VIOLENCE AND VICE.. YOU KNOW, RICK..

TV GUILE

STAN LYNDÉ

..MOSTLY CHILDREN'S SHOWS.

© 1961 by The Chicago Tribune.

1-26

LET'S WATCH THAT THERE ADULT EASTERN, CHIEF..

TV GUILE

YOU KNOW, WHERE THEM FELLERS GO AROUND FIGHTIN' CRIME, MACHINE-GUNNIN' FOLKS, AN' WRECKIN' BREWERIES!

OH, YES.. THE UNMENTIONABLES.

THAT'S THE ONE! BOY, THAT SHOW'S GOT ACTION!

IT CERTAINLY HAS..

KLIK!

..IT MAKES OUR FIGHT WITH CUSTER LOOK LIKE AN OLD LADIES' TEA!

STAN LYNDE

© 1961 by The Chicago Tribune.

THEM UNMENTIONABLE FELLERS SHORE DO WANT YOU ARRESTED, DON'T THEY?

YEP.. IN A WAY, AH WISH AH COULD OBLIGE 'EM.

IT DOES SEEM SORTER IMPOLITE T' REFUSE.. THEM BEIN' BIG CITY PEACE OFFICERS AN' ALL..

YEAH.. BUT AH SHORE HATE BEIN' ARRESTED BY STRANGERS.

STAN LYNDE

'COURSE, AH WOULDN'T MIND IF YOU LOCKED ME UP, RICK.. THAT'D BE DIFFER'NT..

..YO'RE MAH FRIEND!

© 1961 by The Chicago Tribune.

OH! BITTER IRONY! HERE I AM..JAILED BY THE MARSHAL I APPOINTED!

© 1961 by The Chicago Tribune.

NOW I KNOW HOW DOCTOR FRANKENSTEIN MUST HAVE FELT WHEN..

GOOD NEWS, DEUCES!

STAN LYNDE

I RECKON YO'RE PLUM TIRED O' SETTIN' IN THAT CELL ALL ALONE..

RICK! YOU MEAN.. I'M TO BE FREED?

NOT EXACTLY.. BUT I BRUNG YOU SOME COMPANY!

HOWDY, TINHORN!

YES, SIR, MR. MESS.. I LOCKED OL' HIPSHOT UP.. LIKE YOU SAID.

WELL, IT'S ABOUT TIME.

STAN LYNDE

FRANKLY, MARSHAL, I WAS BEGINNING TO DOUBT YOUR COMPETENCE AS AN OFFICER OF THE LAW..

..BUT I'M GLAD TO SEE I WAS WRONG. NOW.. WHERE ARE YOUR CELL KEYS?

© 1961 by The Chicago Tribune.

HERE Y' GO, SPORT!

DO YOU MEAN YOU LEFT THE KEYS IN THE CELL WITH YOUR PRISONERS?

WELL.. YEAH. RECKON I DID.

GOOD HEAVENS, MARSHAL.. DO YOU ALWAYS DO THAT?

OH, NO, SIR, MR. MESS.. ONLY WHEN THEY'S MY FRIENDS!

USUALLY, I'VE GOT COLD-BLOODED KILLERS.. OUTLAWS AN' SUCH.. IN THERE.. DES'PRIT STRANGERS!

© 1961 by The Chicago Tribune.

WHY, I'D BE CRAZY T' LEAVE THE KEYS IN THERE WITH CRIM'NALS!

STAN LYNDE

AFTER HIM, MEN! WE MUST **APPREHEND** THAT DELINQUENT!

RRRRRRROWRRR!

THE UNMENTIONABLES PURSUE THE FLEEING QUYAT.

© 1961 by The Chicago Tribune.

4-3

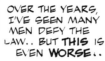

OVER THE YEARS, I'VE SEEN MANY MEN DEFY THE LAW.. BUT **THIS** IS EVEN **WORSE**..

.. THAT CHILD DEFIED **ME**!

STAN LYNDE

4-4

STAN LYNDE

Meanwhile, the Natives are Restless.

PEACE AN' QUIET.. HEAP **NO GOOD**!

ME! GREATEST FIGHTIN' MAN SINCE **GERONIMO**.. BIGGEST **TROUBLEMAKER** SINCE **KHRUSHCHEV**.. UNEMPLOYED.

MY TOMAHAWK IS DUSTY, MY SCALPIN' KNIFE IS RUSTY, AN' I AIN'T KILLED A SINGLE PALEFACE THIS YEAR..

© 1961 by The Chicago Tribune.

.. OR A **MARRIED** ONE, EITHER.

4-5

A FINE CHIEF YOUR FATHER IS, MOONGLOW.. HE'S RUINED MY LIFE!

HOW'S THAT, CRAZY?

HE WON'T LET US BRAVES KILL PALEFACES NO MORE.. HE SAYS GOOD WILL **PAYS** BETTER..

.. YOU KNOW, **PEACEFUL COEXISTENCE** AN' ALL THAT JAZZ. I'VE EVEN FORGOT PROPER **SCALPIN'** TECHNIQUE!

© 1961 by The Chicago Tribune.

I GUESS I'LL JUST HAVE TO GET A NEW **HOBBY**.

STAN LYNDE

4-6

SINCE YOUR OL' MAN DECLARED **PEACE** ON THE PALEFACES, LIFE HAS BEEN A DRAG, BABY.

I WISH **I** WAS CHIEF.. **I'D** SHOW THEM COTTON-PICKIN' PALEFACES!

I GUESS YOU **ARE** CHIEF RIGHT NOW, CRAZY.. DADDY'S **GONE**.

HIS T.V. SET BROKE DOWN AND HE TOOK IT IN FOR **REPAIRS**.

YEAH? WHAT'S **WRONG** WITH IT?

STAN LYNDE

© 1961 by The Chicago Tribune.

I DON'T KNOW FOR SURE.. BUT LAST NIGHT **LORETTA YOUNG** RAN THE AQUANAUTS OUT OF DODGE CITY!

Corporal Jubal Lee

Among the topics receiving national attention during 1961 was the Centennial of the American Civil War. Books, articles, television and film documentaries, as well as reenactments of famous battles, were among the ways Americans observed the event. It has been said that the polarities of the Civil Rights movement and the nation's growing involvement in the Viet Nam War gave added meaning to our national introspection regarding the War Between The States and I am certain that is so. However, as a cartoonist in need of a story, I turned to the creative technique that seemed to work so well for me and again asked myself "what if."

What if a confederate soldier was sent out on a secret mission during the Civil War, fell into a deep sleep a la Rip Van Winkle, and awoke in 1961? And *what if* he became involved with Rick and the people around Conniption? And *what if* he came upon a reenactment, in progress?

Incidentally, Corporal Jubal Lee was a temporary character, appearing in only one story in the strip, but I later gave his name to a permanent character--the pastor of the church in Conniption. Who knows? Maybe the preacher was a *descendent* of the corporal.

5-3

THE CAPTAIN GAVE ME MAH ORDERS.. TO SEEK OUT A YANKEE OUTPOST NAMED FORT CHAOS..

..AH WAS TO NOTE TROOP STRENGTH, FORTIFICATIONS, AN' SUCH.. AN' REPORT BACK T' HEADQUARTERS.

SO AH DREW SOME SUPPLIES FOR MAH JOURNEY..

..AN' MAH COMRADES HELPED ME GET STARTED!

© 1961 by The Chicago Tribune.

STAN LYNDE

5-4

YOU SAY THE CONFEDERATE ARMY SENT YOU HERE TO SPY ON FORT CHAOS?

THAT'S RIGHT, DAUGHTER.. BUT AH RUN INTO TROUBLE.

TWO DAYS OUT O' CAMP, AH NOTICED AH WAS RUNNIN' LOW ON SUPPLIES..

AH HAD NO CHOICE.. AH HAD T' SACRIFICE MAH MULE..

..AN' CONTINUE ON FOOT.. STEADFAST AN' UNSWERVIN'!

STAN LYNDE

© 1961 by The Chicago Tribune.

5-5

AH KEPT A-TRUDGIN' ON TOWARD FORT CHAOS.. BUT AGAIN, MAH SUPPLIES WAS RUNNIN' LOW..

THEN.. SUDDEN-LIKE.. AH COME TO A INJUN CAMP! A YOUNG MEDICINE MAN WELCOMED ME..

FLASH IN THE PAN MEDICINE MAN POTIONS - CURES HEXES - HOME BREW

HEAP CHEAP!

..AND SOLD ME FRESH SUPPLIES!

STAN LYNDE

© 1961 by The Chicago Tribune.

5-6

AFTER AH LEFT THE INJUN CAMP, AH SAMPLED SOME O' THE MEDICINE AH'D BOUGHT..

STAN LYNDE

..BUT AH SEEMED T' GET POWERFUL DROWSY. FINALLY, AH FOUND ME A CAVE.. AN' FELL ASLEEP.

..AN' THAT'S WHERE AH'VE BEEN.. 'TIL YOU WOKE ME UP.

YOU SAY ALL THIS WAS IN 1863?

© 1961 by The Chicago Tribune.

YOU CERTAINLY SHOULD FEEL RESTED!

27

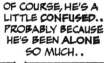

5-22

AH KNOWS THEY'S A LITTLE DIFFERENCE IN OUR AGES, HONEY GAL.. ABOUT A HUNNERD YEARS..

..BUT AH CAIN'T HE'P MAHSELF, DARLIN'.. AH'M PLUM CRAZY ABOUT Y'ALL!

YOU..YOU ARE? BUT, JUBAL..YOU HARDLY KNOW ME!

STAN LYNDE

WELL..THEY'S NOTHIN' LIKE MARRIAGE T' GET FOLKS ACQUAINTED!

© 1961 by The Chicago Tribune.

5-23

THAT'S RIGHT, GAL.. AH'M PROPOSIN' AT Y'ALL! LET'S GET HITCHED RIGHT AWAY!

I'M TERRIBLY FLATTERED, JUBAL.. HONESTLY..

STAN LYNDE

..BUT IT JUST ISN'T POSSIBLE!

WHY NOT? YOU ALREADY HITCHED?

NO, THAT'S NOT IT.. BUT I LOVE ANOTHER!

OH, IS THAT ALL? SHUCKS, THAT AIN'T NO PROBLEM!

© 1961 by The Chicago Tribune.

LEASTWAYS, IT WON'T BE.. AFTER THE DUEL!

5-24

YOU MEAN YOU INTEND TO FIGHT A DUEL OVER ME?

YEP.. AH AIN'T GOT TIME T' MESS AROUND, GAL..

STAN LYNDE

YOU CAIN'T MARRY UP WITH ME ON ACCOUNT O' YORE LOVIN' ANOTHER MAN.. RIGHT?

YES, BUT..

WELL, THEN.. WE'LL SETTLE THE MATTER IN THE GRAND OL' TRADITION O' THE SOUTH..

..PISTOLS FOR TWO.. AN' COFFEE FOR ONE.

© 1961 by The Chicago Tribune.

5-25

GAYE! YOU ALL RIGHT?

RICK!

WHEN YOUR HORSE CAME IN WITHOUT YOU, I 'MOST WENT LOCO WITH WORRY!

OH, RICK..

I'M ALL RIGHT NOW THAT YOU'RE HERE.. YOU NEEDN'T WORRY ANY MORE.

ON THE CONTRARY, GAL..

STAN LYNDE

© 1961 by The Chicago Tribune.

..HIS WORRIES ARE JUST BEGINNIN'!

31

6-9

NOW YOU MEN IN THE CONFEDERATE UNIFORMS ARE TO ATTACK THE FORT FROM THE SOUTH..

THE REST OF YOU WILL FIRE FROM THE RAMPARTS UNTIL THE ATTACKERS ARE REPULSED.

VERY WELL, THEN.. TAKE YOUR PLACES. WHAT?!

© 1961 by The Chicago Tribune.

JUST USE THE BLANK CARTRIDGES, REILLY.. NO AD-LIBBING!

STAN LYNDE

6-10

MEANWHILE, JUBAL GETS RESTLESS..

AH CAIN'T WAIT NO LONGER..AH'VE GOT TO COMPLETE MAH MISSION.

NAMELY, T' FIND THAT YANKEE FORT. IT MUST BE AROUND HERE SOMEWHERES..

© 1961 by The Chicago Tribune.

STAN LYNDE

6-12

STAN LYNDE

FORT CHAOS! WELL, AH DECLARE.. AH'VE FINALLY FOUND IT! AN' JES' IN TIME, 'PEARS LIKE..

© 1961 by The Chicago Tribune.

..THEM BOYS IS CONFED'-RITS..MAH COMRADES.. AN' THEY'S FIXIN' T' ATTACK!

'COURSE, THEY AIN'T VERY MANY OF 'EM.. THEY DON'T HAVE MUCH CHANCE O' WINNIN'..

HOLT ON, FELLERS.. WAIT FO' YO' REINFORCEMENTS!

6-13

The sham attack on Fort Chaos opens with a REAL Rebel Yell!

THEM FELLERS PLAYIN' CONFED'RITS AIN'T TURNIN' BACK LIKE THEY'RE S'POSED TO, GEN'RIL.

THEY WILL, RICK.. THEY KNOW THEY'RE SUPPOSED TO LOSE.

BESIDES, THERE'S NO DANGER. BOTH SIDES ARE FIRING BLANKS.

STAN LYNDE

SPANG!

© 1961 by The Chicago Tribune.

Spirit Drum

Another way to build suspense in a story is to create a supernatural, infallible means of predicting future events and then (gasp!) spring an unthinkable prophecy on the reader. I did just that in the summer of 1961 with the legend of the Spirit Drum, and the prophecy *"Hipshot Percussion Will Die!"*

The readers knew, of course, that I wouldn't *really* kill off the strip's most popular character ("He *wouldn't* do that, would he?"). Still, I had set up the premise--the prophecy of the Spirit Drum *always* comes true"--and the prediction of Hipshot's death was plain and unequivocal.

This story was neither the first nor the last time I placed Hipshot in harm's way. Neither, to paraphrase Mark Twain's famous comment, was it the last time reports of the gunslinger's death were greatly exaggerated. *"Hipshot Percussion Will Die!"* said the drum, and the prophecy of the drum is never wrong.

Now, thirty-four years later, I find the infallible prediction may be fallible indeed. Nothing lasts forever, of course, but thanks to fans, Rickies, and to reader loyalty that has extended even unto the present generation, it sometimes seems (almost) that Hipshot may *never* die.

6-23

SO OL' JUBAL LEE GO 'WAY ON IRON HORSE, EH?

YEP, FLASH.. HE'S HEADED HOME.. TO THE SOUTH.

I GUESS I BETTER GET HOME MYSELF.. I GOT MANY STUFF TO DO.

SURE YOU CAN'T STICK AROUND FOR SUPPER? I'M BUYIN'!

I'D LOVE TO, RICK.. BUT I'LL HAVE TO EAT AT HOME..

© 1961 by The Chicago Tribune.

..I FORGOT T' BRING MY TEETH!

STAN LYNDE

6-24

I GUESS BBIN' MEDICINE MAN OF THE KYUTES KEEPS YOU PURTY BUSY, FLASH..

YOU KNOW IT, RICK.. TAKE TOMORROW, FOR EXAMPLE..

STAN LYNDE

I GOTTA MIX TWO LOVE POTIONS, DRIVE OUT A EVIL SPIRIT, AN' PERFORM A APPENDECTOMY.

SOUNDS LIKE A SHORT HIST'RY OF THE HUMAN RACE.

AN' THAT AIN'T ALL, EITHER.. I'VE JUST DEVELOPED A NEW CURE..

© 1961 by The Chicago Tribune.

..AN' NOW I GOTTA FIGURE OUT A DISEASE FOR IT.

6-28

WHY DON'T YOU COME OUT TO THE RESERVATION AN' HAVE SUPPER WITH ME, RICK?

WHY, MUCH OBLIGED, FLASH..MEBBE I WILL.

YOU'LL HAVE T' TAKE POT LUCK, THOUGH.. I AIN'T SURE WHAT WE'RE GONNA HAVE.

MY SQUAW MAKES GOOD MEALS, BUT SOMETIMES THE INGREDIENTS IS KINDA SPOOKY.

THAT DON'T SCARE ME.. I'VE GOT A REAL HANDY PHILOSOPHY..

STAN LYNDE

..ENJOY LIFE..AN' DON'T ASK TOO MANY QUESTIONS!

© 1961 by The Chicago Tribune.

6-27

HOOOEE! THAT WAS SOME MEAL, FLASH!

YES.. THE LITTLE WOMAN CAN COOK, ALL RIGHT.

AS A MATTER OF FACT, THAT'S THE REASON I MARRIED HER.

STAN LYNDE

© 1961 by The Chicago Tribune.

WE'VE HAD A VERY HAPPY MARRIAGE, RICK..THANKS TO HER ATTITUDE!

HER ATTITUDE?

YEP.. HER GREAT RESPECT FOR HER ELDERS.

39

6-28

SOON NOW COMES THE TIME OF THE ANNUAL PREDICTION.. THE PROPHECY OF THE SPIRIT DRUM.

SPIRIT DRUM?

YEP.. EACH YEAR ABOUT THIS TIME THE SPIRITS SPEAK THROUGH THE DRUM.., FORETELLING THE FUTURE.

© 1961 by The Chicago Tribune.

AND EACH YEAR -- WITHOUT FAIL -- THE PROPHECY COMES TRUE.

WHY, THAT'S WONDERFUL, FLASH!

THE WAY THINGS ARE TODAY, IT'S COMFORTIN' JES' KNOWIN' THEY'S GONNA BE A FUTURE!

STAN LYNDE

6-29

YOU SAY THIS ANNUAL PROPHECY OF THE SPIRIT DRUM ALWAYS COMES TRUE?

ALWAYS HAS, RICK.

ONCE EACH YEAR I TALK TO SPIRITS.. AND THE PREDICTION APPEARS.. WRITTEN ON THE DRUMHEAD.

WELL, I DECLARE!

STAN LYNDE

OH, IT'S FLASHY ALL RIGHT, BUT IT DOES HAVE ITS DRAWBACKS..

© 1961 by The Chicago Tribune.

..MAINLY, THAT THERE'S NO WAY O' KNOWIN' IN ADVANCE WHAT THE PROPHECY'LL BE!

6-30

THE PROPHECY OF THE SPIRIT DRUM NEVER FAILS.. BUT IT ONLY HAPPENS ONCE A YEAR.

AN' YOU CAIN'T TELL AHEAD O' TIME WHAT'LL BE PREDICTED?

NOPE. LAST TIME, FOR EXAMPLE, AFTER WAITING ALL YEAR, THE PROPHECY FINALLY CAME

© 1961 by The Chicago Tribune.

..IT SAID ALASKA WOULD HAVE SOME SNOWFALL DURING JANUARY.

STAN LYNDE

7-1

Sunrise...

THE SIGNS ARE RIGHT, RICK.. I GO NOW TO SPEAK WITH THE SPIRITS.

BY DOGIES! THIS IS EXCITIN'!

JES' THINK, FLASH.. THEY'S FOLKS THAT DON'T BELIEVE A FELLER CAN TALK T' SPIRITS.

THAT'S TRUE.. I DON'T KNOW IF I BELIEVE IT MYSELF.

© 1961 by The Chicago Tribune.

BUT I'VE ALWAYS BEEN ABLE TO, SO I GUESS THEY BELIEVE IN ME!

STAN LYNDE

40

41

7-26

BARNEY! LOOK!

HUH?

THAT GRAY GELDIN' IN THE CORRAL..THAT'S HIPSHOT'S HOSS!

I'D KNOW THAT BRONC ANYWHERES. HIPSHOT'S HERE IN TOWN, ALL RIGHT.

UH..YOU THINK HE'LL BE HERE LONG?

YEP. MATTER O' FACT, I DON'T THINK HE'LL EVER LEAVE.

7-27

NICE JOB, BARBER.. NOW IF AH TAKE ME A BATH, AH'LL LOOK ALMOST HUMAN.

IT'S BACK THERE, FRIEND.. THERE'S HOT WATER ON THE STOVE.

IT'S HIPSHOT ALL RIGHT, SLICK.. HE JUST GOT A SHAVE AN' HAIRCUT!

GETTIN' SPRUCED UP, IS HE? WELL, THAT'S GOOD..

HE'LL LOOK REAL NICE AT THE BURYIN'.

7-28

NOW HERE'S HOW WE'LL WORK IT, BARNEY.. YOU'LL BE DOWN BEYOND THE BARBER SHOP..

..AN' I'LL BE HERE IN THE STREET. WHEN HIPSHOT COMES OUT, I'LL CALL HIM OUT..

..HE'LL DRAW ON ME AN' WE'LL CUT HIM DOWN IN THE CROSSFIRE. GOT IT?

UH.. YEAH, SLICK.. IF YOU SAY SO..

..BUT IT DON'T SEEM VERY NICE.

7-29

I'M STEPPIN' OUT FOR SOME COFFEE, PETE.. KEEP AN EYE ON THE SHOP, WILL YOU?

THAT BIG FELLER BACK THERE IN THE BATH IS PAID UP. HE'LL BE LEAVIN' SOON.

THIS SHORE IS PLEASURESOME.. AH'M SHORN, SHAVED AN' SHAMPOOED, AH'LL SOON BE HOME..

..AN' AH AIN'T GOT A WORRY IN THE WORLD.

8-9

CARE TO CONTRIBUTE TO THE HIPSHOT MEMORIAL FUND, RICK?

THE WHICH? WHAT IN TARNATION IS A HIPSHOT MEMORIAL FUND?

WHAT IS IT? WHY, IT'S A FUND FOR THE PURCHASE OF A SUITABLE MONUMENT TO THE MEMORY OF ONE OF CONNIPTION'S MOST ADMIRED AND RESPECTED CITIZENS, TO WIT: OUR DEAR AND LATELY DEPARTED FRIEND, HIPSHOT PERCUSSION!

STAN LYNDE

SORRY I ASKED.

8-10

THAT'S RIGHT, RICK..THROUGH THEIR GENEROUS CONTRIBUTIONS, HIPSHOT'S FRIENDS HAVE PROVIDED HIM A GREAT MEMORIAL!

Y'MEAN SOME KIND O' STATUE?

PRECISELY! I BOUGHT IT MYSELF. COME.. I'LL SHOW YOU!

STAND BACK NOW WHILE I UNVEIL IT. READY?

I CAIN'T HARDLY WAIT!

STAN LYNDE

VOILÀ!

8-11

THERE IT IS, RICK.. A GREAT MEMORIAL TO A GREAT MAN!

THAT'S S'POSED T'BE A STATUE O' HIPSHOT?

OF COURSE! CAN'T YOU SEE THE RESEMBLANCE?

WELL.. I S'POSE.. IF YOU SAY SO..

..BUT IF I DIDN'T KNOW THAT THING WAS A GREAT MEMORIAL..

STAN LYNDE

..I'D SWEAR IT WAS A SEEGAR STORE INJUN!

8-12

OH, THIS IS THE BALLAD OF HIPSHOT PERCUSSION.. WHO WASN'T A RICH MAN WITH OIL WELLS A-GUSHIN'..

STAN LYNDE

HE WAS KIND TO THE WOMENFOLK, FULL OF GOOD CHEER.. 'TIL HE FELL BY THE SIXGUN OF THAT VARMINT SLICK SNEER!

IF HIP HAD KNOWED FOLKS WOULD CARRY ON LIKE THIS, HE'D NEVER'VE WENT!

8-18

LEAVING TOWN, RICK?

YOU JUS' BETCHA!

STAN LYNDE

I'M PLUM' FED UP WITH FOLKS TRADIN' ON HIPSHOT'S NAME, CLAIMIN' THEY WAS HIS FRIENDS..

I'VE HAD A BELLYFULL O' CROCODILE TEARS AN' BALLADS AN' DIME NOVELS AN' SUCH!

THE ONLY THING WRONG WITH THIS WORLD IS THE PEOPLE!

© 1961 by The Chicago Tribune.

8-19

HEY, RICK! WAIT FOR ME!

LILY!

© 1961 by The Chicago Tribune.

I KNOW WHY YO'RE LEAVIN'.. IT'S 'CAUSE YOU CAIN'T STOMACH THEM HIPPYKRITS BACK THERE EITHER!

THE WAY THEY'RE GRIEVIN' OVER THAT MISER'BLE POLECAT, HIPSHOT! I KNOW HOW YOU FEEL, RICK..

STAN LYNDE

I LOVED HIM, TOO.

8-21

MISS GAYE.. WHY DON'T RICK GO AFTER THAT VARMINT WHO SHOT HIPSHOT?

HE'D LIKE TO, QUYAT.. BUT HE CAN'T.

RICK IS A LAWMAN.. AND AS SUCH HE HAS TO ACCEPT THE LAW'S VERDICT..

STAN LYNDE

..THE LAW CALLED THE SHOOTING SELF-DEFENSE.. SO THERE'S NOTHING RICK CAN DO.

NOPE. I RECKON HIS HANDS ARE TIED, ALL RIGHT..

© 1961 by The Chicago Tribune.

BUT THERE AIN'T NO ROPES ON MINE.

8-22

I RECKON IT'S UP T'ME T' GET EVEN FOR OL' HIPSHOT..

© 1961 by The Chicago Tribune.

I'LL FIND THAT FELLER SLICK SNEER WHO KILT HIM AND HAVE A SHOWDOWN.

STAN LYNDE

LET'S SEE.. DO I HAVE EVERYTHING? FUDGE AN' PICKLE SANDWICH, TWO MARBLES, MY RABBIT'S FOOT..

I SHORE WISH I WAS OLD ENOUGH TO TAKE A GUN.

8-28

WHAT? QUYAT'S GONE TO RAMPAGE?

THAT'S WHAT SASSY FRASS SAYS.. SHE SAW HIM LEAVE.

I'VE GOT T' STOP HIM BEFORE HE GETS THERE.. THAT TOWN'S PURE POISON!

FULL OF OUTLAWS AN' RENEGADES.. THIEVES AN' KILLERS..

IT'S REALLY THAT BAD?

STAN LYNDE

WELL.. ALL I KNOW IS LAST YEAR THE RATTLESNAKES MOVED OUT!

© 1961 by The Chicago Tribune.

8-29

Meanwhile, in Rampage.

YEP, JACK.. WHEN YOU SENT US T' GET HIPSHOT, YOU SHORE PICKED THE RIGHT FELLERS.

I AGREE, SLICK.. I'M MOST PLEASED.

BOYS LIKE YOU ARE A RARE THING IN THE HIRED KILLER TRADE.. YOU'VE GOT INTEGRITY.

BUT HOW ABOUT HIPSHOT'S FRIENDS? ANY CHANCE OF THEM COMING HERE FOR REVENGE?

NOT LIKELY.. A MAN LIKE HIM DON'T HAVE MANY FRIENDS..

STAN LYNDE

© 1961 by The Chicago Tribune.

BESIDES, WHO'D DARE COME AFTER US?

8-30

WHICH ONE O' YOU POLECATS IS SLICK SNEER?

HUH?

WELL, NOW.. I AM, SONNY.. BUT THAT AIN'T NO WAY T' TALK T' YORE ELDERS.

YOU AIN'T MY ELDER.. YOU'RE A YELLER-BELLIED SNAKE! DRAW!

YO'RE A LIPPY LITTLE WHELP AIN'CHA? I GOT A NOTION T' WARM YORE BRITCHES..

HE'S JES' PLAYIN' GUNFIGHTER, SLICK.. GO AHEAD.. DRAW FOR HIM.

WELL.. ALL RIGHT..

STAN LYNDE

THUNK!

© 1961 by The Chicago Tribune.—

8-31

HOLY SMOKES! THE KID GOT SLICK.. WIT' A SLINGSHOT!

I JES' SORTER ROCKED HIM T' SLEEP, THAT'S ALL.

THIS HAS GONE FAR ENOUGH.. GRAB HIM, BARNEY!

NOW AREN'T YOU ASHAMED? YOU SHOULDN'T BOUNCE ROCKS OFFEN GROWNUPS, BOY.

UH.. YEAH! THAT'S RIGHT!

© 1961 by The Chicago Tribun.

WHY DON'CHA PICK ON SOMEBODY YORE OWN SIZE?

STAN LYNDE

53

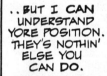

57

I SWAN, HIP.. FOLKS THOUGHT YOU'D BEEN KILT!

NOT AS AH KIN RECALL, RICK..

9-25

..LEASTWAYS, AH'M AS LIVE AS USUAL.

BUT, WHAT HAPPENED? PLENTY O' FOLKS SAW THE SHOOTIN'.. HOW..?

FOLKS DID SEE A SHOOTIN' THAT DAY, TRUE.. BUT IT WARN'T ME WHO CASHED IN.

RECKON AH JES' WARN'T IN THE MOOD.

© 1961 by The Chicago Tribune

STAN LYNDE

AH WAS IN THE BACK OF THE BARBERSHOP, HAVIN' ME A BATH THAT DAY, RICK..

9-26

AH'D HUNG MAH GUNS AN' CLOTHES OUTSIDE THE DOOR AN' WAS SOAKIN' OFF THE TRAIL-DUST..

STAN LYNDE

..WHEN SUDDEN-LIKE, AH HEARS SOMEBODY OUT IN THE HALL..MESSIN' WITH MAH CLOTHES..

BATH →

WELL, I SWAN! Y'MEAN SOMEBODY WAS ROBBIN' YOU FER A CHANGE?

© 1961 by The Chicago Tribune

STEPPIN' OUT O' THE BATHTUB.. AN' NEKKID AS A JAYBIRD.. AH EASE OPEN THE DOOR..

9-27

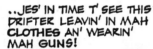

..JES' IN TIME T' SEE THIS DRIFTER LEAVIN' IN MAH CLOTHES AN' WEARIN' MAH GUNS!

I DECLARE! DIDN'CHA TRY AND STOP HIM?

WELL.. AH WEREN'T EXACTLY DRESSED FER PURSUIT.

STAN LYNDE

© 1961 by The Chicago Tribune

SO THIS DRIFTER STOLE YORE CLOTHES AN' GUNS WHILE 'YOU WAS TAKIN' A BATH?

YEP..

9-28

..AN' WHEN SLICK SNEER SEEN HIM, HE FIGGERED IT WAS ME AN' GUNNED HIM DOWN!

PORE FELLER.. AN' ALL BECAUSE HE STOLE YORE GEAR..

YEP.. LIKE AH ALLUS SAY.. CRIME JES' DON'T PAY.

STAN LYNDE

© 1961 by The Chicago Tribune

59

9-29

WHEN AH LEARNED THAT EVER'ONE THOUGHT AH'D BEEN KILLED, AH DECIDED T' LAY LOW AWHILE..

AH KNOWED THE GAMBLERS'D FIGGER THEY WAS SAFE WITH ME DEFUNCT.

SO YOU TOOK T' HOLDIN' UP THEIR GAMES AGAIN, HUH?

WELL, PARD.. SEEIN' AS YO'RE A LAWMAN.. LET'S PUT IT THIS WAY..

..AH DID SOLICIT A FEW CONTRIBUTIONS FER THE POOR.

STAN LYNDE

© 1961 by The Chicago Tribune.

9-30

DON'T MOVE, MR. OUTLAW.. OR I'LL MASSAGE YORE NOGGIN WITH THIS SHOVEL!

YOU DON'T SCARE ME, KID..

..THERE'S NOTHIN' THAT LIVES KIN SCARE BARNEY KLOD! I'M.. HUH?

STAN LYNDE

YIIIIII!

© 1961 by The Chicago Tribune.

RECKON HE DON'T FIGGER AH'M SOMETHIN' THAT LIVES!

10-2

A GHOST! A GHOST!

STAN LYNDE

I DECLARE! BARNEY LEFT HERE LIKE A TAIL-CANNED DOG! SEEIN' YOU SHORE SPOOKED HIM!

H-HIPSHOT! IS IT REALLY YOU?

THERE, THERE, BOY.. EVERTHIN'S ALL RIGHT.. OL' HIP UNNERSTANDS...

AH'VE GOT SOMETHIN' IN MAH EYE, TOO.

© 1961 by The Chicago Tribune.

10-3

RIDE ON IN AN' TELL FOLKS THE GOOD NEWS, QUYAT.. WE'LL BE ALONG LATER.

SURE, RICK!

CONNIPTION 1 MILE

←DIRECTLY→

WELL, FLASH IN THE PAN? I THOUGHT YORE SPIRIT DRUM PROPHECY NEVER FAILED..

..IT PREDICTED THAT HIP WOULD DIE, REMEMBER? EXPLAIN THAT, YOU SLIPPERY VARMINT!

IS TRUE.. PROPHECY NEVER FAIL, IT SAY HIPSHOT WILL DIE..

STAN LYNDE

..AND I IMAGINE HE WILL.. SOONER OR LATER.

© 1961 by The Chicago Tribune.

Dear Libby

What does a big-time advice-to-the-lovelorn columnist do when her syndicated column starts to slip? Well, according to the Dear Libby story from late 1961, she resorts to a publicity ploy which takes her from New York to Conniption in an attempt to solve the romantic dilemma of the Kyute tribe's war chief, Crazy Quilt.

The strip's focus in those early years was humor--satire, farce, slapstick, humor in all its forms. In this story I played culture shock for all it was worth, and scrupulously followed *Moon Mullins* creator Frank Willard's advice to cartoonists: "Throw funny at 'em with both hands."

Panel 10-18:

THAT'S THE STORY, RICK..MOONGLOW WON'T MARRY UP WITH ME 'CAUSE I AIN'T **CIVILIZED.**

THAT'S A **SHAME,** CRAZY QUILT..BUT WHAT KIN I **DO?**

MOONGLOW NUTS FER **CIVILIZATION**..SO I GOTTA **GET** SOME! I WANT YOU TELL ME **HOW!**

GAWRSH, CRAZY.. THAT'S A LITTLE OUTTA MY **LINE**..

STAN LYNDE

..IT'S MOSTLY **EDUCATED** FOLKS.. POLITICIANS, DIPLOMATS AN' SUCH..THAT SAVVY **CIVILIZATION.**

SAME FELLERS THAT KEEP TALKIN' ABOUT **WAR?**

© 1961 by The Chicago Tribune.

Panel 10-19:

I'D LIKE T' HELP YOU OUT, CRAZY QUILT..BUT I SHORE AIN'T NO **ROMANCE** AUTHORITY.

UNDERSTANDIN' ROMANTIC PROBLEMS IS A CAREER IN ITSELF. FOLKS EVEN **WRITE** ABOUT IT IN **NEWSPAPERS..**

STAN LYNDE

TAKE THIS LADY IN THE *SHEBANG SENTINEL*.. "DEAR **LIBBY**".. SHE'S ALLUS ADVISIN' FOLKS!

NO **FOOLIN'?** HOW MUCH IT **COSTS?**

THE SHEBANG SENTINEL

© 1961 by The Chicago Tribune.

NOT A **THING,** CRAZY.. ADVICE IS THE CHEAPEST THING THERE **IS!**

Panel 10-20:

HOW THIS "DEAR LIBBY" **SOLVES** FOLKS' PROBLEMS, RICK?

LEMME READ FROM THIS COLUMN HERE..

Dear Libby

LADY SAYS, "DEAR LIBBY.. I AM IN LOVE WITH A MARRIED **MAN.** IS THAT **WRONG?**"

ROBBERS ESCAPE   PRES TO SEEK GOP AID

..AN' LIBBY ANSWERS AN' SAYS "NO, NOT IF IT'S YORE **HUSBAND!**"

STAN LYNDE

YOU SURE YOU AIN'T READIN' THE **COMICS?**

Panel 10-21:

HERE'S ANOTHER LETTER, CRAZY QUILT.. "DEAR LIBBY," IT SAYS, "I AM 8 FEET TALL AN' WEIGH 75 POUNDS..

..AN' SEEM UNATTRACTIVE TO **MEN.** TELL ME, DEAR LIBBY..WHAT CAN I **DO?**" SIGNED "LONELY."

WHAT DO LIBBY ADVISE **HER?**

JAIL

QUICKER'N A FLASH, SHE SOLVES THE PROBLEM! "FERGIT MEN," SHE SAYS, "GO OUT FER **BASKETBALL!**"

STAN LYNDE

© 1961 by The Chicago Tribune.

10-27

MOE, DAHLING.. I JUST GOT YOUR MESSAGE.. YOU WANTED TO SEE ME?

AS A MATTER OF FACT, I DID, LIBBY.. SIT DOWN.

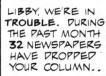

LIBBY, WE'RE IN TROUBLE. DURING THE PAST MONTH 32 NEWSPAPERS HAVE DROPPED YOUR COLUMN..

STAN LYNDE

YOUR STUFF HAS LOST ITS ZING, LIBBY.. THE READERS HAVE LOST CONFIDENCE IN YOU!

RIDICULOUS, DAHLING.. THE NAME LIBBY MAUDLIN IS A HOUSEHOLD WORD!

© 1961 by The Chicago Tribune.

SO, MY DEAR, IS "GARBAGE."

10-28

THIS IS SERIOUS, LIBBY.. WE HERE AT FATUOUS FEATURES HAVE A FINANCIAL INTEREST AT STAKE!

UNLESS YOUR COLUMN IMPROVES, YOU'RE THROUGH.. AND WE GET A NEW LIBBY!

DON'T BE ABSURD, DAHLING.. WHO ELSE COULD TAKE MY PLACE?

STAN LYNDE

EVERYONE KNOWS I'M THE AUTHORITY ON LOVE, MARRIAGE AND ALL THAT ROT..

© 1961 by The Chicago Tribune.

..AFTER ALL, I HAVE BEEN MARRIED SIX TIMES!

10-30

THINGS ARE DESPERATE, LIBBY.. EVERY DAY BRINGS MORE CANCELLATIONS OF YOUR COLUMN.. YOU'RE LOSING YOUR READERS!

NONSENSE.. MY READERS ADORE ME!

STAN LYNDE

WHY, THIS MORNING I EVEN RECEIVED A LETTER FROM AN AMERICAN INDIAN!

HE'S ABSOLUTELY ABJECT BECAUSE THE CHIEF'S DAUGHTER WON'T MARRY HIM.. AND WHO DID HE TURN TO? ME!

WELL.. PLEASE DON'T GIVE HIM ANY ADVICE, LIBBY..

© 1961 by The Chicago Tribune.

..THE INDIANS HAVE BEEN WRONGED ENOUGH AS IT IS!

10-31

WAIT A MINUTE! THAT LETTER! DID YOU SAY IT'S FROM AN AMERICAN INDIAN?

WHY..YES, BUT..

"DEAR LIBBY.. I AM A KYUTE INDIAN BOY WHO LOVES THE CHIEF'S DAUGHTER SOMETHIN' FIERCE."

STAN LYNDE

"..BUT SHE WON'T MARRY ME 'CAUSE I AIN'T CIVILIZED.." LIBBY.. THIS LETTER! IT'S WONDERFUL!

IT IS?

FATUOUS FEATURES SYNDICATE

MOE RALEIGH EDITOR

© 1961 by The Chicago Tribune.

IT CERTAINLY IS! THIS MAY BE ONE TIME A READER WILL SOLVE YOUR PROBLEM!

11-1

THIS LETTER FROM THE INDIAN BOY JUST **MAY** BE THE ANSWER TO OUR **PROBLEM**, LIBBY.

..A LOVELORN INDIAN BOY.. **HEARTBROKEN**.. NEEDING ADVICE.. HE TURNS TO OUR OWN **DEAR LIBBY**..

I MAY BE ILL.

..WHO IS DEEPLY TOUCHED BY THE ROMANTIC CRISIS OF THIS **NOBLE** REDMAN.. THIS **EARLIEST** AMERICAN !

I AM?

MOE, DAHLING.. **YOU** NEED A **REST**.

STAN LYNDE

© 1961 by The Chicago Tribune.

11-2

DON'T LAUGH, LIBBY.. THIS INDIAN BOY MAY BE THE LAST CHANCE TO SAVE YOUR COLUMN.

WE'LL DO A PROMOTION PIECE ON THE CASE.. STRESS THE HUMAN INTEREST ANGLE..

STAN LYNDE

WE'LL SEND YOU.. WITH A PHOTO-GRAPHER.. TO THE KYUTE RESERVA-TION TO **PERSONALLY** SOLVE HIS PROBLEM.

ME? GO TO AN INDIAN RESERVATION? I **WON'T** !

© 1961 by The Chicago Tribune.

SUIT YOURSELF, LIBBY.. IT'S EITHER THE **RESERVATION** OR THE **UNEMPLOYMENT** OFFICE !

11-3

HERE ARE YOUR TICKETS, LIBBY.. AND YOUR LUGGAGE IS CHECKED THROUGH TO DENVER.

I **STILL** THINK THE WHOLE IDEA IS **PREPOSTEROUS**..

STAN LYNDE 2

..ME..LIBBY MAUDLIN..TRAVELING TO SOME HICK HAMLET TO ADVISE AN ABSURD ABORIGINE ON ROMANCE !

IT'S ONLY BECAUSE I RESPECT YOUR **JUDGMENT** SO MUCH THAT I'M GOING AT **ALL**.

IS THAT **REALLY** THE **ONLY** REASON, LIBBY?

© 1961 by The Chicago Tribune.

WELL..YES. THAT.. AND THE FACT MY **LAWYER** SAID I'D **BETTER** !

11-4

ON A DENVER-BOUND JET..

WHAT'S OUR ITINERARY, SAM?

LEMME SEE, MISS LIBBY..

FROM STAPLETON FIELD WE TAKE A RENTAL CAR TO SILVERTON WHERE WE CATCH A **TRAIN** TO CONNIPTION.

WELL..THAT DOESN'T SOUND SO BAD, ANYWAY..

STAN LYNDE

..I **DO** HOPE WE GET A COMFORTABLE **COMPARTMENT** ON THE **TRAIN**.

© 1961 by The Chicago Tribune.

COMPARTMENT?

THERE YOU ARE, MISS LIBBY.. THAT'S ALL OF IT.

THANK YOU SO MUCH, MARSHAL.. THIS IS FOR YOU.

FOUR BITS? BUT.. WHAT FOR, MA'AM?

IT'S A TIP.. FOR CARRYING MY BAGS.

NO, MA'AM.. I COULDN'T. SHUCKS, IT WARN'T NO TROUBLE!

STAN LYNDE

© 1961 by The Chicago Tribune.

NOW THERE GOES A REAL VANISHING AMERICAN!

SO THIS RELIC OF THE DARK AGES IS WHAT YOU CALL A HOTEL, IS IT?

WELL, YEAH, DEARIE.. MORE OR LESS. WHAT'S THE TROUBLE?

TROUBLE? ASIDE FROM NO PLUMBING, KEROSENE LIGHT, A LUMPY MATTRESS AND A ROPE FIRE ESCAPE.. NOT MUCH..

STAN LYNDE

..EXCEPT THAT I PAID FOR A ROOM WITH BATH! I GIVE UP.. WHERE IS IT?

WHY, IT'S RIGHT HERE, HONEY..

© 1961 by The Chicago Tribune.

..WHERE ELSE?

HELLO AGAIN, MARSHAL.. CARE T' JOIN ME? I'M SOAKIN' UP SOME OF YOUR WESTERN ATMOSPHERE.

AMONG OTHER THINGS.

MY USUAL, BILLY. WELL, WHAT DO YOU THINK OF OUR LITTLE TOWN, SAM?

TROOTFULLY, I NEVER SAW A WESTERN TOWN I LIKED MORE..

© 1961 by The Chicago Tribune.

..BUT THEN I'VE NEVER BEEN WEST BEFORE SO MY EXPERIENCE IS LIMITED.

STAN LYNDE

ME FOR SOME SHUT-EYE, SAM.. I'LL SEE YOU FOLKS T'MORRA.

FINE, MARSHAL.. YOU GONNA TAKE US TO THE INDIAN CAMP?

YEP.. I'LL PICK YOU AN' MISS LIBBY UP AT THE HOTEL IN THE MORNIN'.

NOT TOO EARLY, I HOPE.

SALOON

SHUCKS, NO, SAM .. I AIM T' SLEEP LATE MYSELF..

© 1961 by The Chicago Tribune

WHY, I PROBABLY WON'T SEE YOU FOLKS 'TIL 5 A.M.!

STAN LYNDE

5 A.M.
11-20

MISS LIBBY! IT'S SUNUP!

COME ON DOWN AN' I'LL STAKE YOU T' SOME BREAKFAST!

BREAKFAST? AT 5 A.M.?

COULDN'T WE WAIT UNTIL MORNING?

STAN LYNDE

© 1961 by The Chicago Tribune

11-21
GOOD MORNIN', MISS LIBBY!

THAT'S YOUR OPINION..

I'D HEARD THE WEST WAS WILD, BUT GETTING UP AT 5 A.M. IS POSITIVELY BARBARIC!

WHY, WHAT TIME DO YOU USUALLY GET UP?

BACK IN NEW YORK? AT THE EARLIEST, EIGHT O'CLOCK!

WELL, THEY'S NO PROBLEM THEN..

STAN LYNDE

© 1961 by The Chicago Tribune

IT'S THREE HOURS LATER IN NEW YORK, SO REALLY IT IS EIGHT O'CLOCK!

11-22
NOTHIN' LIKE A GOOD BREAKFAST T' START OFF THE DAY, I ALLUS SAY..

I B'LEEVE I'LL HAVE A STEAK, FRIED 'TATERS, SCRAMBLED EGGS, CORNMEAL MUSH, BISCUITS AN' COFFEE.

Bill of fare

CONNIPTION CAFE

IS THAT ALL?

STAN LYNDE

YEP.. SOMEHOW I JES' AIN'T VERY HUNGRY.

© 1961 by The Chicago Tribune

11-23
I SHORE DO LIKE THIS TIME O' DAY, MISS LIBBY..

STAN LYNDE

..THE OL' SUN COMIN' UP, COLORIN' THE SKY.. THE BIRDS AN' CRITTERS COMMENCIN' T' MOVE..

..THE WHOLE WORLD WAKIN' UP! AIN'T IT BEAUTIFUL?

I'LL LET YOU KNOW..

© 1961 by The Chicago Tribune

JUST AS SOON AS I CAN OPEN MY EYES.

72

12-8

YOU SAY YOU KNOW HOW I CAN WIN MOONGLOW? WELL.. SHOOT, KID.. I'M ALL EARS!

IT'S ONE OF THE OLDEST WAYS IN THE WORLD..

..AROUSE HER JEALOUSY.. PRETEND INTEREST IN ANOTHER GIRL!

YOU MEAN I GOTTA ROMANCE SOME OTHER SQUAW?

I GOTTA SPEND MY TIME SMOOCHIN' AN' CARRYIN' ON WITH SOME BEAUTIFUL, YOUNG, FRIENDLY-TYPE BABE?

© 1961 by The Chicago Tribune.

IT'S A TERRIBLE SACRIFICE.. BUT FOR MOONGLOW, I'LL DO IT!

STAN LYNDE

12-9

ALL I GOTTA DO IS START COURTIN' ANOTHER GAL AN' MOONGLOW WILL COME AROUND?

THAT'S MY CONSIDERED OPINION.

SOUNDS GOOD, ALL RIGHT. HMM.. WHO'S GONNA BE THE LUCKY SQUAW?

THAT'S ENTIRELY UP TO YOU, MR. QUILT.

ENTIRELY?

ENTIRELY.

STAN LYNDE

© 1961 by The Chicago Tribune.

HELLO, PALEFACE BABY.

12-11

YOU SAY I SHOULD GET GIRL FRIEND.. MAKE MOONGLOW HEAP JEALOUS.. OKAY, PALEFACE, BABY.. YOU'RE IT!

NOW, MR. CRAZY QUILT.. REALLY!

COME HERE, LUCKY ONE.. CRAZY QUILT ARE FEELIN' ROMANTIC!

I MUST KEEP CALM..

SURELY MY SUPERIOR INTELLIGENCE AND TRAINING ENABLE ME TO CONTROL THIS PRIMITIVE INDIVIDUAL..

..ESPECIALLY IF I CAN OUTRUN HIM!

STAN LYNDE

© 1961 by The Chicago Tribune.

12-12

WHERE CRAZY QUILT, MOONGLOW? I NOT SEE HIM AROUND LATELY.

MAYBE I'VE FINALLY GOTTEN RID OF HIM, DANCING FAWN.

SUDSO DETERGENT

THANK HEAVEN, WHATEVER THE REASON.. AT LEAST HE'S NOT PESTERING ME TO MARRY HIM..

© 1961 by The Chicago Tribune.

WAIT FOR LOVER, PALEFACE BABY!

STAN LYNDE

WELL! HE'S NOT ONLY A PEST.. HE'S UNFAITHFUL!

12-18

OH, I'M **TERRIBLY** SORRY, RICK.. I WAS JUST **PRACTICING.**

UNLESS I WAS THE TARGET, YOU NEED MORE **PRACTICE.**

PRACTICIN' FOR WHAT? DON'T TELL ME YOU LADIES ARE FIXIN' T' **UPRISE.**

NO.. NOTHING LIKE THAT..

.. CRAZY QUILT IS CHASIN' THAT PALEFACE SQUAW, AN' I'M GOING TO **SHOOT** HIM.

SHOOT HIM? DON'T YOU THINK THAT'S A MITE **DRASTIC?**

STAN LYNDE

© 1961 by The Chicago Tribune.

WELL..YES, I SUPPOSE. OKAY THEN.. I'LL SHOOT **HER!**

12-19

YOU CAN'T JES' GO T' SHOOTIN' FOLKS, MOONGLOW.. IT AIN'T HARDLY NICE.. LET ALONE **LEGAL.**

IT'S NO USE, RICK..

..I'M A WOMAN **SCORNED..** AND YOU KNOW WHAT'S GOT NO FURY LIKE A WOMAN **SCORNED.**

WELL, YES, BUT..

THAT TWO-TIMIN' REDSKIN ROMEO HAS GONE TOO **FAR!**

MEBBE SO..

© 1961 by The Chicago Tribune.

..BUT THE MOOD YOU'RE IN SAYS HE'D BEST GO A GOOD DISTANCE **FURTHER!**

STAN LYNDE

12-20

JES' BECAUSE SOMEBODY'S HURT YOUR **PRIDE** IS NO REASON T' GO SHOOTIN' FOLKS, MOONGLOW..

TO A WOMAN, THAT'S REASON **ENOUGH.**

BESIDES, REMEMBER WHAT **KIPLING** WROTE: *"the female of the species is deadlier than the male."*

KIPLING WROTE **THAT?** WELL, I SWAN!

© 1961 by The Chicago Tribune.

I'VE KNOWED OL' JOE KIPLING FOR FIFTEEN YEARS AN' NEVER KNOWED HE COULD **WRITE!**

STAN LYNDE

12-21

ALL RIGHT, MOONGLOW..IF I CAN'T PERSUADE YOU NOT T'GO ON THE WARPATH..

..I'LL JES' HAVE T' SEND FOR YOUR DADDY. HE'LL KNOW WHAT TO DO.

BUT THEY'S ONE THING I KNOW.. YOU CAN'T GO SHOOTIN' FOLKS WILLY-NILLY..

© 1961 by The Chicago Tribune.

THIS HERE IS THE CHRISTMAS SEASON..NOT HUNTIN' SEASON!

STAN LYNDE

Purdy Green

The citizens of Moosemilk (population 17) have long since become resigned to the depradations of outlaw Packy Le Ratt, Scourge of the North. Their relationship with the bandit is monotonously symbiotic--the people are the sheep, Packy is the shearer. The people giveth, and Packy taketh away.

The plot thickens and the balance changes when Rick O'Shay arrives in the area and upsets the status quo. What the marshal of Conniption is seeking is solitude. What he finds is an encounter with the larcenous Packy Le Ratt.

Along the way, Rick also meets a wanna-be Mountie named Purdy Green and Purdy's less-than-heroic dog Bowser as the three embark on an adventure that tests Rick's ingenuity, his patience, and his courage.

Robert Service was right--there *are* strange things done in the midnight sun.

WHAT IN BLAZES IS **WRONG** WITH YOU FOLKS **ANYWAY?**

WHAT'S SO STRANGE ABOUT RIDIN' A **HORSE** OR PAYIN' **CASH** FOR WHAT A FELLER BUYS?

I SWAN, I'M BEGINNIN' T' THINK I'VE RODE INTO A **LAUGHIN' ACADEMY** OR SOMETHIN'!

DON'T MIND US, STRANGER. COME ON IN-SIDE AN' I'LL **EXPLAIN.**

OKAY, BUT THE WAY THINGS HAVE BEEN **GOIN',** SOMEBODY'LL PROB'LY HAVE T' **EXPLAIN** YORE **EXPLANATION!**

SOME TEN YEARS AGO THIS WAS JES' A ORD'NARY TOWN, STRANGER..NO DIFFERENT THAN MOST..

..AN' THEN (SHUDDER!) **PACKY LE RATT..**SCOURGE OF THE NORTH.. MOVED IN AN' TOOK OVER

AN **OUTLAW,** HUH? DIDN'T NOBODY TRY AN' STOP HIM?

O' COURSE WE DID! THERE WAS BRAVE **MEN** HERE THEN.. ME AMONG 'EM!

WELL, THEN.. WHAT HAPPENED?

WHAT **ELSE?** WE DIDN'T WANT OUR BRAVE MEN **KILT,** SO WE GAVE IN!

YOU MEAN THIS WHOLE TOWN HAS LIVED IN FEAR OF ONE OUTLAW FOR **TEN YEARS?**

YEP..HE'S MADE US HIS PRIVATE **HUNTIN' GROUND.**

BUT WHY DO YOU **LET** HIM? IF YOU ALL GOT TOGETHER..

YOU DON'T **KNOW** HIM, STRANGER.. HE'S GOT EVER'BODY SCARED!

WHY, FOLKS HEREABOUTS SPEND HALF THEIR TIME HIDIN' UNDER THEIR BEDS!

THAT'S NO WAY T' LIVE.

MEBBE NOT.. BUT WE'D RATHER BE UNDER THE BED THAN **DEAD.**

WHAT D' YOU FOLKS FIGGER T' **DO..** SPEND YORE WHOLE **LIVES** BEIN' SKEERED O' THIS **OUTLAW?**

I RECKON..HE'S TOO STRONG FOR US.

I THOUGHT THAT WAY ONCE..THERE WAS A BIG KID IN MY SCHOOL..

..HE USED T' WHIP ME EVER' DAY, BUT I KEPT ON FIGHTIN' **BACK..**

UNTIL FINALLY YOU WHUPPED HIM?

NOPE..BUT HE BEGAN T' WORRY THAT I **WOULD** SOME DAY AN' LEFT ME ALONE!

WELL, I'VE GOTTA BE GOIN'! THIS ORTER PAY FOR THE SUPPLIES.

MUCH OBLIGED, STRANGER.. GOOD LUCK.

THIS OUTLAW, PACKY LE RATT, SHORE MUST BE A TERROR.. BUT IT'S NONE O' MY AFFAIR.

STAN LYNDE

I COME UP HERE T' BE ALONE AN' I AIN'T AT ALL INTERESTED IN THEIR LOCAL BADMEN.

THAT COULD CHANGE, RICK!

WE MADE CAMP NONE TOO SOON, TANGLEFOOT..LOOKS LIKE A STORM COMIN' THIS WAY.

THIS SHORE IS LONESOME COUNTRY.. THERE PROB'LY AIN'T ANOTHER HUMAN IN THIRTY MILES..

HMM.. RECKON THIS STEW NEEDS A LITTLE MORE..

STAN LYNDE

..SALT?

© 1962 by The Chicago Tribune.

Bon soir, M'sieur...I SEE SMOKE OF YOU FIRE.. I THEENK MAYBE YOU LOST, non?

SHUCKS NO, STRANGER.. I AIN'T LOST..

I JES' MADE CAMP HERE AN' DECIDED T' FIX ME SOME SUPPER. WOULD YOU..

MERCI BIEN! I WEEL BE MOS' HAPPY FOR JOIN YOU!

© 1962 by The Chicago Tribune.

AH! Le STEW! SHE SMELL MAGNIFIQUE! SHE TASTE magnifique!

GOBBLE SLURP! GULP!

YEAH..WELL, BUT.. I..

STAN LYNDE

WHY FOR YOU DON' EAT, MY FREN'? AIN'T YOU HONGRY?

AH! Merveilleux! YOU ARE MOS' EXCELLENT COOK, mon ami (URP!)..

..BUT YOU SHOULD EAT, TOO. ONE NEEDS FOOD IN THEES NORTH COUN-TRY..n'est-ce pas?

GOOD IDEA, EXCEPT YOU ET IT ALL.

STAN LYNDE

WHAT? I 'AVE EAT YOUR FOOD, TOO? NOM DE NOM! I 'AVE COMMIT FAUX PAS!

OH, THAT'S ALL RIGHT.. I CAN COOK SOMETHIN' ELSE.

TRÈS BIEN! BUT THEES TIME, PUT IN A LEETLE MORE SALT..HOKAY?

© 1962 by The Chicago Tribune.

YOU MEAN THAT TRUNKFUL OF THEATER PROPS IS ALL YOU'VE GOT LEFT?

YEP.. SOME SHOW-FOLK LEFT IT IN TRADE FER A SALAMI SANDWICH.

3-30

BUT I NEED SUPPLIES.. FOOD.. AMMUNITION.. I NEED.. *!

STAN LYNDE

THEATER PROPS, HUH? ON SECOND THOUGHT, I'LL TAKE 'EM..

© 1962 by The Chicago Tribune.

..THEY MIGHT BE JUST THE THING T' BRING DOWN THE CURTAIN ON PACKY LE RATT!

MARTIN & FABBRINI

3-31

WAKE UP, PURDY! WE'RE GOIN' AFTER PACKY LE RATT!

HUH?

HITCH BOWSER TO THE SLED AGAIN.. THIS PACKAGE HERE IS GONNA CATCH US A BANDIT!

RIGHTO, RICK.. THE MOUNTIES ALWAYS GET THEIR MAN!

THAT'S THE SPIRIT, PURDY.. FOLLER THEM TRACKS, BOWSER!

STAN LYNDE

HMM.. I WONDER IF AN IMITATION MOUNTIE ALWAYS GETS HIS MAN..

© 1962 by The Chicago Tribune.

4-2

THERE IT IS, PURDY.. PACKY'S HIDEOUT!

WE'VE FOUND IT!

STAN LYNDE

THANKS TO THEM TRACKS HE LEFT, NOW ALL WE HAVE T'DO IS CATCH HIM.

..AN' THAT'S WHERE THIS PACKAGE COMES IN.. THIS HERE'S OUR SECRET WEAPON.

© 1962 by The Chicago Tribune.

AIN'T IT A BEAUT?

4-3

A HORSE COSTUME? THAT'S GOING TO HELP US CAPTURE PACKY LE RATT?

YEP.. PACKY'S GOT A WEAKNESS FOR HORSES..

..SO WE PUT THIS OUTFIT ON AN' MOSEY AROUND UP HERE ON THIS RIDGE..

© 1962 by The Chicago Tribune.

..HE'LL SEE US AND THINK WE'RE A NEW HORSE FOR HIS COLLECTION.

YEP.. HE'LL COME RIDIN' UP AN' BINGO! WE'VE GOT HIM!

STAN LYNDE

ER.. YES. BUT WHAT IF BINGO! HE GETS US?

101

MARSHAL O'SHAY.. MR. GREEN.. WE OF THE MOUNTED POLICE DEEPLY APPRECIATE WHAT YOU'VE DONE.

YOU'VE CAPTURED OUR MOST WANTED CRIMINAL.. PACKY LE RATT.. AND WE'RE MOST GRATEFUL.

DOES THAT MEAN YOU'LL ACCEPT MY ENLISTMENT NOW?

I'M AFRAID NOT. YOU STILL DON'T MEET OUR QUALIFICATIONS.. BUT I CAN GRANT A FAVOR..

© 1962 by The Chicago Tribune.

..WE WON'T PROSECUTE YOU FOR ILLEGALLY WEARING OUR UNIFORM!

STAN LYNDE

4-19

WELL, PACKY'S IN JAIL AN' I'VE GOT MY HORSES BACK.. RECKON I'LL BE HEADIN' HOME.

BARRACKS B RCMP

STAN LYNDE

I'M SORRY THE MOUNTIES STILL WON'T LET YOU JOIN UP, PURDY.

OH, THAT'S ALL RIGHT, RICK.. I'VE CHANGED MY MIND..

..I DIDN'T REALLY WANT TO BE A MOUNTIE ANYWAY. NOW I HAVE A NEW AMBITION..

© 1962 by The Chicago Tribune.

..TO BECOME LORD OF THE JUNGLE.. LIKE IGNATZ OF THE GORILLAS!

4-20

RECKON I ORTER STOP BY AN' SAY HELLO T' THE FOLKS IN MOOSEMILK..

THEY'LL LIKELY WANT T' THANK ME FER CATCHIN' PACKY LE RATT AN' FREEIN' THEIR TOWN FROM FEAR..

STAN LYNDE

..THEY'LL PROB'LY CALL ME A HERO AN' CARRY ON SOMETHIN' FIERCE..

HOWDY THERE, FRIEND.. REMEMBER ME?

© 1962 by The Chicago Tribune.

I SHORE DO. YOU DERN MEDDLER!

4-21

YOU AIN'T WELCOME IN THIS TOWN, STRANGER, SINCE YOU CAPTURED PACKY LE RATT!

I'M NOT?

NO, YOU AIN'T! WHO ASKED YOU T' COME IN HERE AN' TAKE OUR BANDIT AWAY?

BUT.. BUT HE WAS ROBBIN' YOU BLIND! HE..

© 1962 by The Chicago Tribune.

SURE HE WAS.. AN' NOW WE GOT EVER'THING BACK. BUT IT AIN'T THE SAME..

..WITH HIM GONE, THERE AIN'T NO EXCITEMENT IN LIFE NO MORE.. AN' IT'S ALL YOUR FAULT!

STAN LYNDE

105

Making Up

The cartoonist's job is to entertain, and one of the ways he/she does that is to hold a mirror up to life. That mirror reflects our image, often in a distorted and exaggerated way, like a mirror in a Fun House, but we smile with recognition as we see ourselves--and others we know--on the comics page of our daily newspaper.

It has been truly said that the course of true love (or any other kind) seldom or never runs smooth. Certainly that premise seems always to have been a part of the popular wisdom, and I have no doubt that it always will be.

Misunderstandings lead to hurt feelings, over-reaction, and alienation. Reconciliation begins with self-examination, recognition of our own fault in the matter, and apology.

In the case of Rick and Gaye, their conflict is settled and their closeness restored when they both, simultaneously, admit their error.

Do I believe in mutual apology? You bet I do. Making up can be terriffic.

4-24

I WISH RICK HADN'T **RESIGNED** AS MARSHAL, HIPSHOT.. HE'LL BE DIFFICULT TO **REPLACE**.

AH NEVER KNOWED YOU THOUGHT SO **HIGH** OF HIM, DEUCES..

OH, I **DO**! HE WAS **EFFICIENT**, **CAPABLE**, **HONEST**, **INDUSTRIOUS**, **INTELLIGENT**..

WHAT YO'RE TRYIN' T' SAY IS..?

NOBODY ELSE WOULD DO THE JOB FOR SUCH A SMALL SALARY.

STAN LYNDE

4-25

WELL, IT GOES AG'IN MAH **PRINCIPLES**.. BUT AH MIGHT BE AVAILABLE AS MARSHAL..

STAN LYNDE

..THAT IS, IF RICK **DON'T** WANT THE JOB NO MORE.

GOOD HEAVENS! YOU.. A MARSHAL?

AN' WHY **NOT**, TINHORN?

OH..NO REASON..

..IT'S JUST THAT ONE SELDOM **SEES** A **WOLF** WORKING AS A **SHEEPDOG**.

4-26

BLACK-DANG THE CORN-SWOZZLIN', HIGH-BINDIN'..

KLANK!

IS SOMETHING **WRONG**, HIPSHOT?

OH.. HOWDY, MISS GAYE..

IT'S OUR TINHORN **MAYOR**, DEUCES WILDE..HE SHORE KIN MAKE A FELLER **MAD**.

WHY? WHAT DID HE DO TO **OFFEND** YOU?

WULL.. **FIRST** OFF, HE GOT **BORN**.

STAN LYNDE

4-27

WHY ARE YOU SO ANGRY WITH DEUCES, HIPSHOT?

ME..ANGRY? SHUCKS, AH AIN'T ANGRY..

..AH'M JES' TEMPTED T' BLAST HIM OUT FROM UNDER HIS BEAVER **HAT**, THAT'S ALL.

BUT WHAT HAS HE **DONE**?

HE **INSULTED** ME..AH **THINK**. HE SAID AH WOULDN'T BE A GOOD TOWN **MARSHAL**.

AND **YOU** THINK YOU **WOULD**?

WULL..**NO**. BUT BEIN' **TRUE** DON'T MAKE IT ANY LESS INSULTIN'!

STAN LYNDE

4-28

IT'S REALLY **MY** FAULT THAT WE DON'T HAVE A TOWN MARSHAL, HIPSHOT..

..IF I HADN'T SAID THOSE TERRIBLE THINGS TO RICK, HE'D NEVER HAVE GONE AWAY.

WULL.. IT'S **HIS** FAULT, **TOO**.. FER NOT UNDER-STANDIN' YOU..

WHEN YOU SAID YOU NEVER WANTED T' **SEE** HIM AG'IN, HE **MISUNDERSTOOD** YOU..

WHEN A GAL IN LOVE SAYS "NEVER" SHE **USUAL** MEANS "NOT 'TIL LATER."

STAN LYNDE

© 1962 by The Chicago Tribune.

4-30

I'VE BEEN SUCH A FOOL.. IF ONLY RICK WOULD COME BACK.. LET ME **EXPLAIN**..

NOW DON'T FRET, GAL.. HE'LL BE BACK ..AH KNOW RICK.

HE'LL COME RIDIN' BACK ANY DAY NOW.. SO QUIT **WORRYIN'** ..HEAR?

I'LL TRY ..THANKS, HIPSHOT.

NOW WHY'D I GO AN' SAY THAT? AH AIN'T **NEAR** AS SURE AS AH **SOUNDED**..

RICK! BOUNCIN' BUCKSHOT! AH'M A DERN **PROPHET**!

STAN LYNDE

© 1962 by The Chicago Tribune.

5-1

STAN LYNDE

RICK, YOU OL' **VARMINT**.. YO'RE **BACK**! WHERE'VE YOU **BEEN**, BOY?

I'LL TELL YOU ALL ABOUT IT LATER, HIP..

..BUT RIGHT **NOW** I'VE GOT T' FIND **GAYE**. I HAVE T' TELL HER SOMETHIN'!

EASY DONE, PARD.. SHE'S OVER T' THE CAFE.

ER.. UH.. GAYE?

RICK!

I'M SORRY, HONEY.. I WAS WRONG!

© 1962 by The Chicago Tribune.

5-2

HMM.. MEBBE AH ORTER MOSEY OVER T' THE CAFE AN' SEE WHAT'S **HAPPENIN'**..

STAN LYNDE

RICK AN' GAYE BOTH HAVE PURTY HOT **TEMPERS** SOMETIMES 'AN' SOMEBODY **COULD** GET HURT.

WULL.. AH RECKON **THAT** WON'T DO NO **PERMANENT** DAMAGE.

108

SO.. YOU DECIDED TO COME **BACK**, DID YOU?

YEP.. I'M HOME TO STAY, DEUCES.

5-3

IF YOU'LL GIVE ME THAT **STAR** NOW, I'LL GO BACK T' BEIN' **MARSHAL** AGAIN.

NOT SO **FAST**, RICK..

STAN LYNDE

DURING YOUR ABSENCE, I FOUND THAT OUR NEED FOR LAW ENFORCEMENT WAS LESS GREAT THAN I'D **THOUGHT**..

© 1962 by The Chicago Tribune.

HOWEVER, YOU'RE WELCOME TO THE JOB.. BUT IT NOW PAYS **$30 LESS** PER MONTH.

5-4

SO IF I TAKE MY JOB AS MARSHAL BACK, I GET PAID **$30 LESS**?

THAT'S RIGHT.. TAKE IT OR LEAVE IT.

I CAN'T **ARGUE** WITH YOU, DEUCES.. YOU'RE A HEAP BETTER WITH WORDS THAN I AM..

..IN FACT, I RECKON THE ONLY WAY I CAN ANSWER YOU AT **ALL**..

STAN LYNDE

..IS WITH **ACTION**!

RAPP!

© 1962 by The Chicago Tribune.

5-5

YOU.. YOU **STRUCK** ME! HOW **COULD** YOU?

EASY, TINHORN.. GET UP AN' I'LL **DEMONSTRATE**!

OFFERIN' ME MY JOB BACK AT A CUT IN PAY.. WELL, YOU CAN **KEEP** IT!

STAN LYNDE

BUT I AM SORRY I **HIT** YOU LIKE THAT..

© 1962 by The Chicago Tribune.

..I COULD'VE DONE **BETTER** WITH MY **RIGHT** HAND!

5-7

YOU MEAN DEUCES WOULDN'T GIVE YOU BACK YOUR JOB AS MARSHAL?

OH, HE WAS WILLIN' T' GIVE IT BACK, ALL RIGHT..

..BUT HE FIGGERED T' PAY ME $30 A MONTH LESS FOR DOIN' IT.

WHAT ARE YOU GOING TO DO, RICK?

STAN LYNDE

MEBBE GO BACK T' COWBOYIN'.. OR SIGN ON AS DEPUTY OVER T' SHEBANG..

I AIN'T WORRIED, ANYWAYS.. A FELLER KIN MAKE A FAIR LIVIN' THESE DAYS BEIN' UNEMPLOYED!

© 1962 by The Chicago Tribune.

Kyute Movie

Movies fired my imagination early, and my interest in the medium has only grown greater with the passage of time. As a kid, growing up on the Crow Indian reservation in southeast Montana, the movies brought visions of different worlds and exotic places, and they portrayed heroic men and beautiful women in dramatic and exciting adventures.

The westerns, especially, captured my interest. The "A" westerns were grand (and sometimes pretentious); the "B" westerns, with their guitar-strumming, singing heroes and their intelligent and amazing horses, were wholesome; and the "C" westerns were--well, it was often a tough call, but in general I thought they were better than no westerns at all.

There were ironies, though. Old-time cowboys--the genuine article--men who had come up the cattle trails from Texas and who had lived their entire lives in the saddle watched some of the least authentic western movies with fascination and nary a word of complaint. Indian children sat on the edges of their seats and, like the rest of us, cheered for Duke Wayne and the cavalry, finding nothing much in Hollywood's portrayal of their ancestors to excite them.

Those images, and the memory of the many films which portrayed the Indian culture and people poorly, led in 1962 to the Kyute Movie story. Once again, cultures collide as Conniption meets Hollywood, and as Chief Horse's Neck gives his all in an effort to balance the scales, set the record straight, battle injustice, and, of course, make himself a buck.

5-8

HOWDY, CHIEF.. WHAT'S **NEW**?

NOT **MUCH**, RICK..

..EXCEPT THAT I'M CONSIDERING DECLARING **WAR** ON THE **UNITED STATES**.

WHAT?!

ARE YOU PLUM' **LOCO**? WHY, YOUR LITTLE KYUTE TRIBE COULDN'T **HOPE** TO WIN!

OH, I KNOW **THAT**, RICK

STAN LYNDE

I'M RATHER HOPING WE'D **LOSE**.

SHEBANG SENTINEL, May 8, 1962

West Germany, Japan, Italy Enjoy Record Prosperity

Washington, May 7 (LP) - Economists said today that the nations which made up the World War II...

5-9

WHEN THE WHITE MAN CAME, WE **FOUGHT**.. AND, ONE WAY OR THE OTHER, WE **LOST**.

WE LOST OUR **BUFFALO**, OUR **LAND**, OUR WAY OF LIFE.

STAN LYNDE

FINALLY, ALL WE HAD LEFT TO CALL OUR OWN WERE THE **MOON** AND **STARS** ABOVE..

.. AND **NOW** YOU COTTON-PICKIN' PALEFACES ARE GOIN' AFTER **THEM**!

5-10

MY PEOPLE ONCE LIVED **HAPPY, SIMPLE** LIVES, RICK ..HUNTING, FISHING, **KILLING** THEIR **NEIGHBORS**..

BUT NOW, ALL IS CHANGED. **SHOPPING CENTERS** STAND TODAY WHERE GREAT **BUFFALO** HERDS ONCE ROAMED.

WHEN I THINK OF HOW YOU PALEFACES HAVE CHANGED THIS COUNTRY..

STAN LYNDE

..I GET SO DEPRESSED I CAN HARDLY ENJOY MY FAVORITE **TELEVISION** SHOWS!

5-11

DO YOU WATCH MUCH T.V., CHIEF?

AS MUCH AS I CAN **STAND**, RICK.

..I'VE CURRENTLY BECOME INTERESTED IN THE **MEDICAL** SHOWS.. OR **TRAUMA DRAMAS**. BY GEORGE, THEY'RE EXCITING!

DOCTORS ARGUING WITH THEIR **WIVES**, FIST-FIGHTING WITH **CRIMINALS**.. **SMOOCHIN'** IN THE CORRIDORS, NEGLECTING THEIR **PATIENTS**..

THESE SHOWS CERTAINLY MAKE A PERSON GLAD HE'S **HEALTHY**.

STAN LYNDE

LYMPH LUMBAR, M.D.

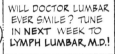

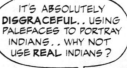

5-22

COULD BE YOU'RE BEIN' A MITE **HARD** ON THEM MOVIE PRODUCERS, CHIEF..

STAN LYNDE

MEBBE THEY USE WHITE FOLKS IN INJUN PARTS FOR A GOOD **REASON.**

SO! YOU'RE **DEFENDING** THEM, ARE YOU? I MIGHT HAVE KNOWN..

..ONCE A PALEFACE, **ALWAYS** A PALEFACE!

© 1962 by The Chicago Tribune.

5-23

THERE'S ONLY ONE THING TO DO, RICK.. I MUST GO TO HOLLYWOOD **MYSELF.**

© 1962 by The Chicago Tribune.

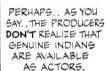

PERHAPS.. AS YOU SAY.. THE PRODUCERS **DON'T** REALIZE THAT GENUINE INDIANS ARE AVAILABLE AS ACTORS.

IN THAT CASE I'LL BE ABLE TO SHOW THEM **LIVING PROOF** THAT THEY **ARE**..

STAN LYNDE

..MY TWO STALWART BRAVES.. **CRAZY QUILT** AND **BUTTERCUP!**

5-24

YOU AIM T' TAKE **CRAZY QUILT** AN' **BUTTERCUP** TO HOLLYWOOD?

CERTAINLY! WHY SHOULDN'T I?

PAPA NEEDUM NEW MOCCASINS!

COME SNAKES EYE!

OH.. NO REASON, I RECKON. IT'S JUST THAT FROM WHAT I'VE HEARD OF **HOLLYWOOD**..

STAN LYNDE

..THEY'VE GOT PLENTY O' SCREWBALLS **ALREADY!**

© 1962 by The Chicago Tribune.

5-25

I ONLY WISH I **KNEW** SOMEONE IN THE MOVIE INDUSTRY.. WE'LL NEED **CONNECTIONS.**

YEAH.. I S'POSE.. **HEY!** I KNOW SOMEBODY.. **TOM FOOLERY!**

SNAP!

© 1962 by The Chicago Tribune.

BY GEORGE, YOU'RE **RIGHT!** TOM **IS** STILL ON THE COAST, ISN'T HE?

HE SHORE **IS**.. WE WRITE EACH OTHER REGULAR..

..AN' HE'D BE **GLAD** T' HELP OUT.. IF HE HAS **TIME.** HE WORKS PRETTY **HARD.**

STAN LYNDE

MORE GRAPES, HONEY..

114

THESE BOYS IS **FRIENDS O'** MINE, MAGNUM.. RICK O'SHAY AN' CHIEF HORSE'S NECK.

HOW DO YOU DO? WON'T YOU SIT DOWN?

6-19

NOW.. WHAT MAY I DO FOR YOU, GENTLEMEN?

I'M HERE ON BEHALF OF **MY PEOPLE,** MR. MOGUL..

STAN LYNDE

I'VE COME TO INQUIRE **WHY** REAL INDIANS AREN'T USED TO PORTRAY INDIANS ON THE SCREEN.

IN OUR **PIONEERING** DAYS THEY **WERE,** CHIEF..

.. BUT **TODAY'S** AUDIENCES SEEM TO PREFER OUR **NEW SYNTHETICS!**

© 1962 by The Chicago Tribune.

STAN LYNDE

MOTION PICTURES **DID** USE REAL INDIANS, CHIEF.. FOR MANY YEARS..

6-20

.. BUT TO BE FRANK, THE TIME CAME WHEN THEY'D FORGOTTEN HOW TO **BE** INDIANS.

THEY FORGOT HOW TO **RIDE,** SEND SMOKE SIGNALS, SAY "UGH".. **THEN** CAME THE LAST **STRAW..**

.. I SHOWED ONE AN **ARROW** AND HE SAID, "WHAT'S **THAT** THING, MAN?"

© 1962 by The Chicago Tribune.

WHAT YOU SAY ABOUT INDIANS HAVING FORGOTTEN THEIR TRADITIONAL SKILLS MAY BE TRUE, MR. MOGUL..

6-21

.. BUT I ASSURE YOU THAT SUCH IS **NOT** THE CASE WITH MY PEOPLE, THE **KYUTES.**

SHUCKS, NO.. **THEY'RE** AS SAVAGE AS THEY COME.. EVEN SAVAGER!

THEY'RE **ALLUS** GOIN' ON THE WARPATH.. HOLLERIN', SHOOTIN'.. TAKIN' **SCALPS!**

STAN LYNDE

IT'S GOT SO BAD WE RECOGNIZE **NEWCOMERS** 'CAUSE **THEY GOT HAIR!**

© 1962 by The Chicago Tribune.

I SYMPATHIZE WITH YOUR POSITION, CHIEF.. BUT I HAVE **MY** PROBLEMS, TOO..

6-22

.. RISING PRODUCTION COSTS, TAXES, COMPETITION FROM THE INDEPENDENT PRODUCERS..

I'M **CURRENTLY** MAKING ALL MY PICTURES OUT OF THE COUNTRY IN ORDER TO CUT **COSTS..**

STAN LYNDE

.. AS A MATTER OF FACT, WE'RE **NOW** SHOOTING A **WESTERN** IN HONG KONG!

© 1962 by The Chicago Tribune.

7-7

WE STILL NEED A LEADING MAN FOR OUR MOVIE, TOM.. A BIG NAME.. A STAR!

I KNOW, CHIEF.. WE.. HEY! I KNOW JUST THE FELLER!

SORTER SMOKY LOOKIN' BOY WITH SLICKED DOWN HAIR.. A TANGO DANCER! HE'D BE PERFECT!

AN' HE AIN'T BEEN IN MANY PITCHERS LATELY.. NOW WHAT IS HIS NAME.. RUDOLPH SOMETHIN'..

VALENTINO? GOOD GRIEF, TOM ..HE'S DEAD!

STAN LYNDE

NO FOOLIN'? WHY, I NEVER EVEN KNOWED HE WAS SICK!

© 1962 by The Chicago Tribune   TF

7-9

RICK! I THOUGHT YOU WERE IN HOLLYWOOD!

I WAS, GAYE..

..BUT CRAZY QUILT AN' BUTTERCUP WENT NATIVE AN' UPSET THE CHIEF'S MOVIE DEAL..

..SO HE ASKED ME T' ESCORT 'EM BACK T' THE RESERVATION. BOY, IS HE MAD!

I CAN IMAGINE! HE MUST HAVE THOUGHT THEY'D AT LEAST ACT RESPONSIBLY!

STAN LYNDE

© 1962 by The Chicago Tribune.

YEP..THAT WAS HIS FIRST MISTAKE.

7-10

SO THE CHIEF AND TOM ARE STILL IN HOLLYWOOD?

YEP.. FAR AS I KNOW.

LAST I SEEN OF 'EM THEY WAS RIDIN' OFF INTO THE SUNSET BOULEVARD.. DODGIN' TRAFFIC.

ANYWAYS, I'M SURE GLAD T'BE BACK.. THAT TOWN'S TOO BIG FER ME..

© 1962 by The Chicago Tribune.

WHY, THERE MUST BE A THOUSAND PEOPLE LIVIN' THERE!

STAN LYNDE

7-11

MEANWHILE, BACK IN HOLLYWOOD..

WE MUST HAVE A NAME STAR IN OUR MOVIE, TOM.. TO INSURE BOX OFFICE SUCCESS.

YEAH.. BUT NAME STARS COST MONEY. IF ONLY..

© 1962 by The Chicago Tribune.

HEY! I KNOW A FELLER WHO'D BE PERFECT.. STERLING SILVA!

STAN LYNDE

NOT THE STERLING SILVA!

YEP..AN' WE CAN GET HIM CHEAP, TOO.. HE'S CURRENTLY SUFFERIN' FROM THE STATUS SEEKIN' BLUES.

WHAT IN THE NAME OF GERONIMO IS THAT?

SIMPLE, CHIEF.. THAT'S A ILLNESS FOLKS GET WHEN THEIR OUTGO EXCEEDS THEIR INCOME!

7-17

NOW HOLD ON A MINUTE, STERLING.. IT'S AN ACTIN' JOB WE'RE OFFERIN' YOU!

INDEED?

FORGIVE MY CHILDISH *outburst*, GENTLEMEN.. YOU ARE, THEN, PLANNING TO PRODUCE A *film*?

YEP.. OUR FIRST. WE'D LIKE **YOU** T' **STAR** IN IT!

YOU MEAN YOU'VE NEVER *made* A PICTURE BEFORE? YOU HAVE NO *experience*?

WELL, THAT'S **ONE** WAY T' LOOK AT IT, I RECKON..

..BUT ON THE **OTHER** HAND, WE AIN'T HAD ANY **FAILURES**, EITHER!

© 1962 by The Chicago Tribune.

7-18

VERY WELL.. SINCE I AM TEMPORARILY BETWEEN *engagements*.. AT *liberty*, AS IT WERE.. I *accept*.

I WILL STAR IN YOUR CINEMATIC EXPERIMENT. TELL ME, *where* WILL THE PICTURE BE FILMED?

ON LOCATION, STERLING.. NEAR A LITTLE TOWN CALLED **CONNIPTION**.

© 1962 by The Chicago Tribune.

CONNIPTION, EH? SOME BACKWARD *hamlet* IN THE *hinterlands*, NO DOUBT.. LACKING ALL THE *civilized* *comforts*.

WELL.. IT HAS A SALOON.

Really? ON SECOND THOUGHT IT SOUNDS RATHER *charming!*

7-19

I'M **SO** GLAD YOU AGREED TO STAR IN OUR MOVIE, MR. SILVA!

Naturally. AND WHY *wouldn't* YOU BE?

MY HISTRIONIC *talent* IS EXCEEDED ONLY BY MY GREAT *humility*.

ER.. YEAH, AH'VE **NOTICED**..

WELL.. WE STILL HAVE T' ROUND UP EQUIPMENT AN' TECHNICIANS. WE'LL MEET YOU HERE TOMORROW.

Fear not! I SHALL BE READY AT THE APPOINTED HOUR!

NOW **THERE'S** A BOY WHO MAKES ACTIN' A **FULL-TIME JOB!**

STAN LYNDE

© 1962 by The Chicago Tribune.

7-20

THAT DOES IT, CHIEF.. I'VE RENTED CAMERAS, SOUND TRUCKS, LIGHTS, DOLLIES.. THE **WORKS**.

EXCELLENT, TOM.. NOW ALL WE.. DOLLIES? GOOD HEAVENS!

ACME RENTALS

I NEARLY **FORGOT**.. WE DON'T HAVE A **LEADING LADY**!

DO WE **NEED** ONE?

© 1962 by The Chicago Tribune

OF **COURSE** WE DO.. AND I KNOW **JUST** WHO I WANT.. POLLYANNA PURE!

POLLYANNA PURE!? HOLY **HOSSFEATHERS**, CHIEF.. WHY NOT QUEEN VICTORIA?

DO YOU THINK SHE'D BE INTERESTED?

STAN LYNDE

SORRY, GENTS..BUT **NO DEAL**. I SIMPLY CAN'T AFFORD TO TAKE A CHANCE ON FAILURE.

BUT, MISS PURE.. YOUR FEE WOULD BE PAID IN **ANY** CASE!

7-31

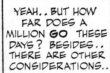

YEAH.. BUT HOW FAR DOES A MILLION **GO** THESE DAYS? BESIDES.. THERE ARE OTHER CONSIDERATIONS..

I HAVE **RESPONSIBILITIES**.. PEOPLE WHO ARE **COUNTING** ON ME TO **REMAIN** A GREAT STAR..

THE INTERNAL REVENUE BOYS, FOR EXAMPLE.

STAN LYNDE

© 1962 by The Chicago Tribune.

8-1

POLLYANNA PURE'S REJECTION OF OUR OFFER **WAS** DISAPPOINTING, TOM..BUT I CAN'T REALLY BLAME HER.

HOWEVER, I **AM** DISAPPOINTED IN HER **PERSONALLY**.. SHE'S NOT AT **ALL** SWEET AND INNOCENT.

SHE **DON'T** EXACTLY LIVE UP TO HER **IMAGE**, DOES SHE?

© 1962 by The Chicago Tribune.

YOU WALKED IN EXPECTIN' A **BUNNY RABBIT**.. AN' MET A **CROCODILE**!

STAN LYNDE

8-2

WELL, THERE'S NO POINT IN **REGRETS**..WE DO HAVE **ONE** NAME STAR FOR OUR MOVIE.

YEP..STERLING SILVA. SHALL I GO PICK HIM UP?

I SUPPOSE. IF THE EQUIPMENT IS READY, WE CAN LEAVE IN THE MORNING.

STAN LYNDE

HOLLYWOOD MAY LAUGH AT US **NOW**.. BUT JUST WAIT! **WE'LL** SHOW THEM!

YOU SHORE GOT **SPIRIT**, CHIEF..

NOT MUCH **JUDGMENT**.. BUT PLENTY O' **SPIRIT**.

© 1962 by The Chicago Tribune.

8-3

TELEGRAM, MARSHAL.. FROM HOLLYWOOD!

IT'S FROM CHIEF HORSE'S NECK, RICK.. HE SAYS HE'LL BE ARRIVIN' ON THE AFTERNOON **TRAIN**!

HE'S BRINGIN' A CREW OF MOVIN' PITCHER FOLKS AND HE WANTS YOU T' **MEET** HIM!

WELL..MUCH **OBLIGED**, PETE..

..ID READ THIS **ALOUD** ONLY IT'S KIND O' **PERSONAL**.

STAN LYNDE

© 1962 by The Chicago Tribune.

ACCORDIN' T' THIS **TELEGRAM**, TOM AND THE CHIEF ARE ARRIVIN' ON THE AFTERNOON **TRAIN**.

YOU MEAN THEY'RE READY TO START FILMING THEIR **MOVIE**?

SEEMS LIKE.. THEY'RE BRINGING ALL THE **EQUIPMENT** AN' A **CREW** O' TECHNICIANS.

A **CREW**? EXCUSE ME, RICK..

STAN LYNDE

HOTEL

© 1962 by The Chicago Tribune.

HOTEL ROOM RATES $5 & UP

STAN LYNDE 8-6

CONNIPTION

13

HOWDY, **CHIEF**! WELCOME **HOME**!

ER.. THANK YOU, RICK..

..BUT WHERE **IS** EVERYONE? I'D RATHER EXPECTED A RECEPTION **COMMITTEE**.

WE KNEW YOU'D FEEL THAT WAY, SO WE DRAWED **STRAWS**..

..AN' **I** GOT T' BE THE **COMMITTEE**!

© 1962 by The Chicago Tribune.

8-7

SEE THAT THE BOYS GET THE EQUIPMENT UNLOADED AND SET UP, TOM..

..THEN SEND THEM OVER TO THE **HOTEL**. I PLAN TO BEGIN **SHOOTING** TOMORROW MORNING.

T'MORRA **MORNIN'**! BUT YOU AIN'T EVEN GOT A **SCRIPT** YET!

© 1962 by The Chicago Tribune.

I KNOW. I'LL HAVE TO WRITE IT THIS **EVENING**.

STAN LYNDE

8-8

GOOD EVENING, DEUCES.. HAS THE PRODUCTION CREW BEEN TAKEN CARE OF?

OH, INDEED THEY **HAVE**, CHIEF..

STAN LYNDE

..EACH MAN HAS RECEIVED BED AND BOARD AT THE RAMSHACKLE HOTEL (CONNIPTION'S FINEST) AT THE **PREVAILING** RATE..

SKIP THE **ORATORY**, MAN..

© 1962 by The Chicago Tribune.

..EXACTLY HOW **MUCH** DID WE TAKE **IN**?

IN BRIEF.. ONE HUNDRED FORTY DOLLARS.

SPLENDID! WE HAVEN'T EVEN STARTED SHOOTING OUR PICTURE AND WE'RE MAKING MONEY **ALREADY**!

8-9

YOUR IDEA OF RAISING PRICES AT THE HOTEL AND CAFE WAS A **CLEVER** ONE, CHIEF..

STAN LYNDE

YOUR PRODUCTION CREW PAYS THE INCREASED RATES, **WE** SPLIT THE **PROFITS**..

..AND **YOU** RECOVER MUCH OF WHAT YOU **PAY** THEM IN **WAGES**! I CERTAINLY HAVE TO **HAND** IT TO YOU!

GOOD IDEA..

© 1962 by The Chicago Tribune.

..SUPPOSE YOU **HAND** ME MY HALF OF THE **MONEY**.

8-10

DON'T THINK I DON'T **TRUST** YOU, DEUCES.. BECAUSE I **DON'T**. I DON'T TRUST **ANY** PALEFACE.

© 1962 by The Chicago Tribune.

..SO I'LL TAKE MY HALF OF THE MONEY **NOW**. THIS IS A SIMPLE BUSINESS DEAL..

STAN LYNDE

MY CREW PAYS FOR ROOM AND BOARD (AT EXORBITANT RATES) AND **WE** SPLIT THE **PROFITS**.

AGREED, CHIEF.. NO COMPLAINTS.

WHOEVER SAID *"Pity the Poor Redman"* **OBVIOUSLY** NEVER MET CHIEF HORSE'S NECK..

HOTEL

8-11

WELL, THE CREW'S **FED**, WATERED AN' **BEDDED DOWN** OVER T' THE **HOTEL**, CHIEF..

SALOON

..BUT **PRICES** HERE HAVE SHORE GONE UP.. THEM **ROOM RATES** ARE HIGHER'N A GIRAFFE'S TONSILS.

THAT'S HOW IT **GOES**, TOM.. **INFLATION** AND ALL THAT.

I S'POSE. HOW'S THAT **SCREENPLAY** COMIN'? YOU BEEN **WORKIN'** ON IT ALL **EVENIN'**.

PRETTY WELL, TOM..

SALOON

STAN LYNDE

© 1962 by The Chicago Tribune.

..I'VE **ALMOST** GOT THE **TITLE**!

8-13

IT'S FINISHED, TOM! THE SCRIPT IS FINISHED!

HUH?

GAD! WHAT A **MOMENT**! THE COMPLETION OF THE SCRIPT FOR THE GREATEST MOVIE EVER **MADE**!

THAT'S NICE.. ONLY WE AIN'T **MADE** IT YET.

IT'S ALL HERE.. THE **DRAMA**.. THE **PATHOS**.. THE **TRAGEDY**.. THE **GREATNESS** OF THE AMERICAN WEST!

ALL **THAT** ON THEM LITTLE BITTY PIECES O' PAPER?

HOTEL

STAN LYNDE

PARD.. HAVE YOU BEEN SAMPLIN' THE **FIREWATER** AGAIN?

© 1962 by The Chicago Tribune.

131

8-14

ALL WE HAVE TO DO NOW IS **CAST** THE PICTURE AND WE CAN BEGIN **SHOOTING!**

I TELL YOU, MAN.. **THIS** WESTERN WILL MAKE MOVIE **HISTORY!** WHY, EVEN THE **TITLE** IS INSPIRED!

ALL RIGHT.. I GIVE UP. WHAT **IS** THE TITLE?

SQUAW MAN SHANE AND HIS HIGH NOON STAGECOACH!

STAN LYNDE

8-15

AS YOU KNOW, RICK, WE'RE USING LOCAL RESIDENTS AS ACTORS IN OUR MOVIE..

HORSE'S NECK

..AND WE'RE CASTING YOU AS SNAKE-EYES, THE **VICIOUS,** SNEERING, COLD-BLOODED PSYCHOPATHIC KILLER.. OKAY?

ME?

GAWRSH, CHIEF.. I AIN'T SURE I CAN **HANDLE** THAT KIND O' PART..

..WHY, I CAN'T EVEN **SNEER!**

STAN LYNDE

8~16

ALL RIGHT, CHIEF.. I'LL PLAY THE VILLAIN IN YORE MOVIE IF YOU **SAY** SO..

STAN LYNDE

..BUT I THINK SOMEBODY LIKE OL' **HIPSHOT** IS MORE THE COLD-BLOODED TYPE.

NONSENSE! YOU'LL BE **PERFECT!** BESIDES, I HAVE **ANOTHER** PART FOR HIPSHOT..

..HE'S GOING TO BE THE **KINDLY,** GENTLE OLD **FRONTIER PREACHER!**

8~17

THE PICTURE OPENS WITH THE WEDDING OF THE HEROINE.. A **BEAUTIFUL,** DELICATE YOUNG EASTERN GIRL..

STAN LYNDE

..PLAYED (NATURALLY) BY MY DAUGHTER, MOONGLOW..

THANKYEW, DADDY.

..AND HER **PURE-HEARTED,** NOBLE YOUNG HUSBAND, PLAYED BY OUR **STAR,** STERLING SILVA..WHERE'S STERLING?

KEEP YER **SHIRT** ON.. WE'RE **BRINGIN'** HIM!

THE CRYSTAL PISTOL SALOON

BAR

8-23

AH NOW PERNOUNCE YOU MAN AN' MISSIZ ..YOU MAY NOW KISS YORE BRIDE.

CUT!

YOU CALL **THAT** A **KISS**? I'VE SEEN **FRENCH GENERALS** HANGIN' **MEDALS** DO BETTER THAN **THAT**! TRY IT AGAIN.. WITH **FEELING**!

STAN LYNDE

WELL, THAT'S **BETTER**!

SHMEERP!

© 1962 by The Chicago Tribune.

8-24

ALL RIGHT.. IN THIS SCENE THE NEWLYWEDS ARE RIDING ACROSS THE PRAIRIE IN THEIR BUGGY..

SUDDENLY, A HORDE OF SAVAGE, HOWLING INDIANS (PLAYED BY MY TALENTED TRIBESMEN) SWOOPS DOWN..

ER.. CHIEF..

BOWSTRINGS HUM! ARROWS WHIZ DANGEROUSLY NEAR! YES? WHAT IS IT CRAZY QUILT?

BIG TROUBLE, CHIEF.

© 1962 by The Chicago Tribune.

NONE OF US KNOW HOW TO SHOOT **BOW** AN' **ARROW**!

STAN LYNDE

8-25

PRODUCTION DIFFICULTIES ARISE..

GERONIMO'S GHOST! SURELY **SOMEBODY** IN THE TRIBE KNOWS HOW TO USE A BOW AND ARROW!

'FRAID **NOT**, O CHIEF.

STAN LYNDE

..WHEN **US** BOYS GO HUNTIN' **NOW'**DAYS, WE USE MIGHTY **THIRTY-OUGHT-SIX THUNDERSTICK** ..POW!

AND YOU CALL YOURSELVES **INDIANS**..

..I OUGHT TO MAKE THE **LOT** OF 'EM TURN IN THEIR **FEATHERS**!

RECKON THERE'S ONLY ONE THING TO **DO**, CHIEF..

CALL IN AN **ARCHERY** EXPERT AS A **TEACHER**.

© 1962 by. The Chicago Tribune.

8-27

OH, THE **SHAME** OF IT! HAVING TO HIRE AN **ARCHERY** EXPERT TO INSTRUCT MY **BRAVES**!

KINDER **IRONICAL**, AIN'T IT?

IT'S **DISGRACEFUL**! MY NOBLE **WARRIORS** ..FORGETTING HOW TO USE THEIR TRADITIONAL WEAPONS!

WHAT HAS HAPPENED TO OUR **CULTURE**? NEXT, THEY'LL FORSAKE OUR ANCIENT CEREMONIAL **DANCES**!

DON'T LOOK NOW, CHIEF..

..BUT **THAT** AIN'T EXACTLY THE **SUN DANCE**!

TWIST, BABY, TWIST!

STAN LYNDE

© 1962 by The Chicago Tribune.

8-28

YOU FIGGER THEM INJUNS HAVE HAD ENOUGH **INSTRUCTION** WITH THE BOW AN' ARROW?

I CERTAINLY **HOPE** SO.. OKAY, LLOYD.

ATTACK SCENE, TAKE FOUR HUNDRED THIRTY-THREE.. **QUIET ON THE SET!**

ROLL 'EM!

WANNNG

..ER..YOU BOYS DON'T **QUITE** HAVE THE KNACK OF IT YET, DO YOU?

STAN LYNDE

8-29

WELL! WE **finally** GOT THE ATTACK SCENE IN THE CAN!

YES, STERLING.. BUT OUR **ARCHERY EXPERT** IS POOPED.

STAN LYNDE

HE HAD TO PLAY THE PART OF **TWENTY** DIFFERENT **INDIANS** AND SHOOT **ALL** THE **ARROWS!**

WELL.. THAT'S *show business.* WHAT'S NEXT?

NEXT IS **YOUR** BIG SCENE, STERLING.. THE JUMP FROM THAT **CLIFF** INTO THE **LAKE.**

What? Good heavens, CHIEF.. I CAN'T EVEN *swim!*

SO.. FAKE IT!

© 1962 by, The Chicago Tribune

8-30

YOU WANT *me* TO MAKE A *two-hundred*-FOOT LEAP INTO THAT *lake?* I *can't!*

WHY NOT?

I *told* YOU, CHIEF.. I CAN'T EVEN *swim!*

OH, DON'T WORRY ABOUT **THAT.**

STAN LYNDE

THAT WATER IS ONLY A FEW INCHES **DEEP!**

© 1962 by The Chicago Tribune.

8-31

FOR THE LAST TIME, I *refuse* TO JUMP OFF THAT CLIFF.. I'M A FANATICAL *coward!*

OH, COME NOW.. THIS SCENE WILL MAKE CINEMA **HISTORY!**

IT WILL ALSO MAKE ME *dead..* HAVE YOU THOUGHT OF *that?*

GOOD HEAVENS.. YOU'RE **RIGHT!** I **HADN'T** THOUGHT OF THAT..

© 1962 by The Chicago Tribune.

WE'LL SHOOT **THAT** SCENE **LAST.**

STAN LYNDE

GOOD NEWS, CHIEF.. **BUTTERCUP** HERE HAS AGREED TO **DOUBLE** FOR STERLING IN THE JUMP SCENE!

SPLENDID!

OKAY, BUTTERCUP.. WHEN YOU HEAR ME SAY "ROLL 'EM," YOU **JUMP.**

STAN LYNDE

ROLL 'EM!

SO MUCH FOR THE **REHEARSAL.** NOW, ONCE AGAIN FOR THE CAMERA!

HOW COME DEUCES IS SO **RICH** ALL OF A SUDDEN, GAYE?

HE'S MADE **SOME** OF IT **GAMBLING** WITH THAT MOVIE CREW..

..BUT THAT **CERTAINLY** DOESN'T ACCOUNT FOR **ALL** HIS NEWFOUND PROSPERITY.

WELL, HE'D BETTER **WATCH** HIMSELF..

THERE'S **SOME** FELLERS HEREABOUTS WHO MIGHT BE **TEMPTED** BY ALL THAT MONEY.

..AH SHOULDA KNOWED.. YOU WAS TEMPTATION..

STAN LYNDE

SALOO

THIS IS THE FINAL SCENE OF THE PICTURE, CAST.. THE **SHOWDOWN** ON **MAIN STREET!**

RICK.. YOU'RE THE VICIOUS KILLER, **SNAKE-EYES.** YOU WALK TOWARD STERLING, YOUR HAND NEAR YOUR GUN..

STERLING.. YOU'RE THE BRAVE, STRONG **HERO.** YOU STAND YOUR GROUND, FEARLESSLY **WAITING.**

.. AND MAY THE **BEST** MAN **WIN.**

STAN LYNDE

POW!

POW!

POW!

STAN LYNDE

CUT! EXCELLENT! THAT WRAPS IT UP.. OUR MOVIE IS **FINISHED!**

BOY, I'M SHORE GLAD YOU WAS ONLY FIRIN' **BLANKS,** STERLING!

BLANKS!

GOOD HEAVENS! I **KNEW** I FORGOT SOMETHING!

Old Rep

The Old Rep story, from the late fall of 1962, proved to be something of a landmark in the life and times of Rick O'Shay. It was among the first, if not *the* first, "straight" adventure story of the many I would produce for the strip over the next 15 years or so, and it provided additional development for the character of Hipshot Percussion.

Early in the strip's life, it had become evident that Hipshot was easily its most popular character, next only to Rick O'Shay himself. Readers had long since become accustomed to Hip's skill with weapons, his courage and coolness under pressure, and his proud lone wolf nature.

Because they had, Hipshot's reaction to word that Old Rep was hunting him caught readers by surprise and heightened the suspense as they awaited the final showdown at sundown on the streets of Conniption.

With the conclusion of the story, the comedy returned, and--as usually happened in my stories--the tale ended on a high note.

NOW THAT YORE MOVIE'S A SUCCESS, I S'POSE YOU'LL BE GOIN' BACK T' HOLLYWOOD, TOM.

NOPE.. I DON'T THINK SO RICK.

I SORTER THOUGHT I'D STAY HERE IN CONNIPTION.. SETTLE DOWN. THIS IS WHERE I BELONG.

WE'LL SURE BE PROUD T' HAVE YOU. BESIDES..

..YORE MOVIN' HERE WILL MEAN A LOT TO THE TOWN.

© 1962 by The Chicago Tribune.

FOR ONE THING, IT'LL RAISE OUR POPULATION A GOOD TEN PERCENT!

STAN LYNDE

WHERE YOU OFF TO, HIP?

BUSINESS TRIP, PARD..

STAN LYNDE

..COWMAN OVER NEAR EAGLE SPRINGS SENT FER ME.. SEEMS HE NEEDS MAH PERFESSIONAL SERVICES.

HIS COWS BEEN DISAPPEARIN' OFF THEIR RANGE LATELY.. LIKE MAGIC, HE SAYS.

WHAT ARE YOU? A SPECIALIST IN MAGICALLY DISAPPEARIN" COWS?

© 1962 by The Chicago Tribune.

NOPE.. IN EXTERMINATIN' MAGICIANS.

I DECLARE, MANUEL..DON'T TELL ME YORE SLEEPIN' ON THE JOB AGAIN?

HOKAY, señor RICK ..I WON'T TELL YOU.

I ONLY DO THEES FOR MY HEALTH. TO TAKE SIESTA EES mucho GOOD FOR ME..NO?

WELL.. YEAH, I S'POSE..

© 1962 by The Chicago Tribune.

STAN LYNDE

YOU UNDERSTAND NOW .. I'M ONLY DOIN' THIS TO PREVENT SICKNESS.

OH, SI.

STATE PRISON

ALL RIGHT, REP..TODAY'S THE DAY. WARDEN WANTS T' SEE YOU.

© 1962 by The Chicago Tribune.

YOU MEAN AH'VE BEEN IN THIS HOLE SEVEN YEARS ALREADY?

MY, HOW TIME DOES FLY!

STAN LYNDE

OLD REP IS OUTSIDE, WARDEN.

SEND HIM IN, JACK

WELL, REP.. THIS IS THE BIG DAY. YOUR SENTENCE HERE AT STATE PRISON IS OVER.

THAT DON'T EXACTLY GRIEVE ME, CLINT.

© 1962 by The Chicago Tribune.

IT'S BEEN A LONG, HARD SEVEN YEARS SINCE THAT GATE CLOSED BEHIND ME.

LONG ENOUGH FOR A MAN TO LEARN HIS LESSON?

WHY, THAT'D DEPEND ON THE MAN, CLINT.. AND ON THE LESSON

STAN LYNDE

10-9

10-10

ACCORDIN' TO THE RULES, THE STATE PROVIDES EACH MAN LEAVIN' THE PRISON WITH CERTAIN ITEMS

HIS PERSONAL EFFECTS, A NEW SUIT AN' TEN DOLLARS. RIGHT?

WELL, YOU GAVE ME MY WATCH, THE TEN-SPOT IS IN MY POCKET AN' I'M WEARIN' THE SUIT

YES.. BUT I'D LIKE TO GIVE YOU ONE THING MORE. REP

STAN LYNDE

IF YOU MEAN ADVICE, CLINT, WE KNOW EACH OTHER TOO WELL FOR THAT.

© 1962 by The Chicago Tribune.

AN IF YOU OFFERED ME ANOTHER SEVEN YEARS ON THE ROCK PILE I'D LIKELY DECLINE.

10-11

STAN LYNDE

WHAT I'M TRYIN' TO SAY REP, IS KEEP OUT O' TROUBLE. YOU'VE DONE YOUR TIME

OH, I KNOW YOU WERE A TOP GUN IN YOUR DAY PROB'LY THE BEST OF 'EM ALL

BUT WHAT DID IT EVER GET YOU? NOTHING!

OH, AH WOULDN'T SAY THAT, CLINT

STATE PRISON

© 1962 by The Chicago Tribune

..IT GOT ME SEVEN YEARS FREE RENT, DIDN'T IT?

STAN LYNDE

10-12

WELL. THERE IT IS ..SHENANIGAN YOU'RE A FREE MAN REP

SORTER HARD T' GET USED TO SOMEHOW

REMEMBER WHAT I SAID, REP. DON'T GO BACK TO PACKIN' A GUN.. GETTIN' IN GUNFIGHTS

AH DON'T AIM TO CLINT

CAFE

STATE PRISON

THESE HANDS ARE STIFF. THEY'RE MORE USED TO SWINGIN' A SLEDGE THAN SLINGIN' A GUN

OK HARD

© 1962 by The Chicago Tribune.

..AN' AH AIN'T PLANNIN' MANY SLEDGE-HAMMER FIGHTS!

10-27

WELCOME TO THE CRYSTAL PISTOL, STRANGER..WHATLL YOU HAVE?

WHUSKY.. AN' INFORMATION.

STAN LYNDE

© 1962 by The Chicago Tribune.

YOU WANT 'EM MIXED OR SEPARATE? I AIN'T GOT MUCH SELECTION OF EITHER COMMODITY.

AH DON'T NEED MUCH OF EITHER ONE, BARKEEP..

AH HEAR TELL THAR'S A MAN HEREABOUTS CALLS HISSELF HIPSHOT.. HIPSHOT PERCUSSION. THAT A FACT?

WHY, YES..THERE IS. YOU A FRIEND OF HIS?

FRIEND? NO, NOT EXACTLY. LET'S JES' SAY AH'VE COME T'SETTLE AN OLD DEBT.

·10-29

LIKE I SAID, STRANGER.. HIPSHOT DOES LIVE HERE IN CONNIPTION, BUT HE'S OUTA TOWN NOW.

HE ALLUS WAS LUCKY. WHEN DO YOU EXPECT HIM BACK?

STAN LYNDE

WELL..THAT'S HARD T'SAY.. A FEW WEEKS.. MEBBE A MONTH.

AH DON'T MIND WAITIN'.. IT'LL GIVE ME TIME T'PRACTICE.

WHERE KIN AH BUY ME A SIX-GUN?

© 1962 by The Chicago Tribune.

10-30

YOU VISH TO BUY A REVOLVER? Das ist Gut. I HAFF MANY FINE VEAPONS IN STOCK.

STAN LYNDE

DIS VUN ISS A GREAT FAVORITE.. SINGLE ACTION .45.

SHOOTS CA'TRIDGES, HUH?

AH DRUTHER HAVE ME A CAP AN' BALL.. AH'M A BLACK POWDER MAN MAHSELF.

BUT DIS VUN ISS DER NEW MODEL..ISS MORE ACCURATE.

MEBBE..BUT AH'VE FOUND MOST GUNS IS ACCURATE..IF THE SHOOTER IS.

© 1962 by The Chicago Tribune.

10-31

AH'LL TAKE THIS'N ..AN' SOME POWDER, BALL AN' CAPS.

Sehr Gut. VOULD YOU LIKE A BELT UND HOLSTER?

CUSTOM BLUEING

NAW..AH'LL TOTE IT IN MAH WAISTBAND. THIS ORTER COVER THE DAMAGES..

STAN LYNDE

Ja Wohl. DO YOU VISH ME TO DEMONSTRATE DER REVOLVER?

MUCH OBLIGED.. BUT THAT WON'T BE NECESSARY..

AH'D BE GLAD TO SHOW YOU A THING OR TWO ABOUT IT, THOUGH!

149

11-6

YESSIR, RICK..THAT FELLER IS **OLD REP**.. A GUNHAWK WITHOUT EQUAL FOR SKILL AN' **COLD NERVE**..

WHY, EVEN A **CONSERVATIVE** GUESS WOULD PUT HIS NOTCHES AT MORE'N **THIRTY**!

WELL, LIKE YOU SAY, TOM.. THAT **WAS** A LONG TIME AGO.

STAN LYNDE

MEBBE HE'S **CHANGED** NOW.. AFTER ALL, HE IS AN OLD MAN.

TRUE ENOUGH, RICK..

© 1962 by The Chicago Tribune.

..BUT WOULD YOU RATHER STEP ON A **OLD RATTLESNAKE** THAN A **YOUNG'UN**?

11-7

LOOKY **HERE**, RICK..THAT OLD WOLF IS BURNIN' POWDER ALL DAY, **EVERY** DAY.. PRACTICIN'.

AN' HE TOLD BILLY THE BARKEEP HE'S WAITIN' FER **HIPSHOT**.. DON'T THAT SORTER ADD UP?

WELL..MEBBE, BUT THAT'S **STILL** JUST SPECULATION.

BLAM!

HOWSOMEEVER, I'LL GO **TALK** TO HIM, ASK HIM WHAT HE'S DOIN' HERE.

UH..YEAH. WELL, IF THINGS DON'T WORK OUT..

STAN LYNDE

..KIN I HAVE YORE **WATCH** AN' CHAIN?

© 1962 by The Chicago Tribune.

11-8

ER..'SCUSE ME, MISTER.. I'M RICK O'SHAY, **MARSHAL** HERE IN TOWN.

HOWDY. AH'M **OLD REP**.

'SO I UNDERSTAND. I ALSO UNDERSTAND YOU'RE **WAITIN'** FOR **HIPSHOT**. THAT TRUE?

YEP.. THAT'S TRUE.

STAN LYNDE

ER.. MEBBE IT'S NONE O' MY **BUSINESS**, BUT WOULD YOU MIND TELLIN' ME **WHY**?

YEP, IT **AIN'T** ANY O' YORE BUSINESS.. AN' YEP **AGAIN**, AH **WOULD** MIND SAYIN' WHY.

© 1962 by The Chicago Tribune.

11-9

RICK..YOU SIMPLY **MUST** DO SOMETHING ABOUT THAT..THAT DESPERADO, OLD REP! HE'S TERRORIZING OUR TOWN!

BY HOLDIN' **TARGET** PRACTICE ON CANS AN' BOTTLES?

SUCH **LEVITY** ILL-BECOMES YOUR **OFFICE**, MARSHAL.. THAT MAN IS A **THREAT** TO OUR **CITIZENS**!

YOU SHORE KNOW HOW T' MAKE MOUNTAINS OUTEN **MOLE HILLS**, DEUCES

SO FAR, HE'S MOSTLY BEEN MINDIN' HIS OWN **BUSINESS**.. AN' THAT AIN'T A CRIME **YET**.

NO? AND JUST **WHY** HAS HE BEEN MINDING HIS OWN BUSINESS?

STAN LYNDE

WANTED JUNIOR WESTWOOD FOR EVERYTHING REWARD

© 1962 by The Chicago Tribune.

BECAUSE HE HAS SOMETHING TO **HIDE**, THAT'S WHY!

151

LOOK, DEUCES.. I CAN'T JAIL THAT OLD MAN FOR WHAT HE MIGHT BE THINKIN'..

MEBBE HE **HAS** COME HERE T' SHOOT IT OUT WITH HIPSHOT.. AN' AGAIN, MEBBE **NOT.**

WHAT ARE YOU GOING TO DO.. JUST **WAIT?**

JUST **WAIT** UNTIL THOSE TWO GUNFIGHTERS **MEET** AND SCATTER LEAD FROM HERE TO THE CITY **LIMITS?**

NO, I AIN'T GONNA JUST WAIT !

© 1962 by The Chicago Tribune.

I THINK I'LL KETCH ME SOME **GRASSHOPPERS** AN' GO **FISHIN'** !

STAN LYNDE

STILL WAITIN' FER HIPSHOT, IS HE ?

I GUESS SO, TOM. HE AIN'T VERY TALKATIVE.

STAN LYNDE

HE JUST COMES IN, HAS ONE DRINK, AN' GOES BACK TO HIS **TARGET** PRACTICE

PORE OLD HIPSHOT.. HE DON'T KNOW WHAT'S **WAITIN'** FOR HIM.

WELL, NOW.. I WOULDN'T WORRY ABOUT HIPSHOT.. HE CAN TAKE CARE OF HIMSELF.

THINK SO?

SKRITCH!

YOU REMEMBER THAT, BILLY.. IT'LL MAKE HIM A FINE EPITAPH.

© 1962 by The Chicago Tribune.

YOU SEEM MIGHTY ALL-FIRED SURE OLD REP CAN TAKE HIPSHOT IN A SHOOT-OUT, TOM.

I AM, BILLY.. I'VE SEEN OLD REP IN ACTION.

MEBBE.. BUT YOU AIN'T SEEN HIPSHOT. I HAVE.. AN' I SAY HE'S THE BEST.

UH-HUH.

BESIDES.. NO MATTER **HOW** GOOD THAT OLD MAN **WAS**, HE'S **OLDER**.. HIS **REFLEXES** ARE SLOWER.

THERE'S JES' ONE LITTLE POINT YOU'RE OVERLOOKIN', BILLY..

STAN LYNDE

..A FELLER HAS T' BE **PURTY** GOOD T' LIVE T' BE·AN **OLD** GUNFIGHTER.

© 1962 by The Chicago Tribune.

I DON'T CARE WHAT TOM SAYS.. THAT OLD MAN WON'T STAND A **CHANCE** AGAINST HIPSHOT.

FOR **PETE'S** SAKE, BILLY.. YOU'RE AS BAD AS DEUCES !

WE DON'T EVEN KNOW THERE'S GONNA BE A SHOOTIN' AN' YOU'RE ALREADY BURYIN' THE LOSER !

I GUESS YOU'RE RIGHT, RICK.. BUT I'VE SORTER COME T' LIKE THE PORE OL' FELLER. BESIDES..

STAN LYNDE

© 1962 by The Chicago Tribune.

..A FELLER DON'T **FIND** A CASH CUSTOMER **EVERY** DAY.

CRACKLE

STAN LYNDE

11-24

COME **OUTA** THERE, HANDS HIGH..WHOEVER YOU ARE!

EASY, HIP..

KLIK!

..SHOOTIN' ME COULD PLUM' RUIN OUR FRIENDSHIP!

RICK!

© 1962 by The Chicago Tribune.

11-26

WHAT BRINGS YOU OUT LOOKIN' FER ME, PARD? YOU LOOK SORTER **WORRIED.**

I **AM,** HIP.

THERE'S AN OLD **MAN** WAITIN' FOR YOU IN CONNIPTION.. WITH A GUN.

IS THAT ALL? SHUCKS, THAT'S NOTHIN' T' WORRY ABOUT..

STAN LYNDE

..FELLERS WITH GUNS BEEN LOOKIN' FER ME ALL MAH **LIFE. SOME** OF 'EM GOT LUCKY..

© 1962 by The Chicago Tribune.

..THEY NEVER CAUGHT UP WITH ME.

11-27

YOU DON'T **UNDERSTAND,** HIP.. THIS FELLER IS A REAL **GUN HAND** ..AN' HE'S HUNTIN' **YOU!**

QUIT **WORRYIN',** RICK..HE **AIN'T** EXACTLY THE **FIRST.**

NOW WHO **IS** THIS OLD FELLER WHO'S SO ANXIOUS T' GET HISSELF SHOT?

ALL I KNOW IS HE CALLS HISSELF OLD **REP,** AN'..

(CHOKE!) OLD REP!

© 1962 by The Chicago Tribune.

HIPSHOT! YOU ALL RIGHT?

STAN LYNDE

11-28

DID..DID YOU SAY **OLD REP** IS L-LOOKIN' FER ME?

WHY..YEAH.. DO YOU **KNOW** HIM?

AH SHORE **DO.** THERE **NEVER** WAS A GUNMAN LIKE **HIM..**HE'S THE **BEST!**

I DECLARE, HIP.. YOU SOUND LIKE YOU'RE **SCARED** OF HIM!

AH **DO?** WELL..IF AH DO, ITS ONLY BECAUSE..

© 1962 by The Chicago Tribune.

STAN LYNDE

..AH **AM.**

155

11-29

I JES' DON'T **UNDERSTAND**, HIP..I'VE NEVER KNOWED **YOU** T' BE AFRAID OF **ANYONE**!

STAN LYNDE

AH AIN'T, RICK.. 'CEPTIN' **HIM**..YOU DON'T **KNOW** HIM!

WELL, **YOU** SURE SEEM TO. HOW COME HE'S **HUNTIN'** YOU, ANYWAYS?

MEBBE IF AH RODE FER THE **BORDER**.. NOW, **TONIGHT** ..MEBBE..

© 1962 by The Chicago Tribune

NAW.. HE'D ONLY **FIND** ME..SOONER OR LATER. AH'VE BEEN RUNNIN' FROM HIM LONG **ENOUGH**.

BESIDES..WE **ALL** HAVE T' GO **SOMETIME**.

11-30

AH'M GOIN' OVER T' THE **HOTEL**, RICK. TELL OLD REP AH'LL MEET HIM COME **SUNDOWN**.

WELL..ALL RIGHT, IF YOU'RE **SURE**.

CONNIPTION

STAN LYNDE

AH'M SURE. THEY'S NO USE RUNNIN' FROM HIM ANY MORE.

I WISH I KNEW WHY HE'S GOT YOU SO **SPOOKED**, HIP.

THAT'S A LONG STORY, PARD. HE'S THE ONLY MAN IN THE WORLD AH'M **SKEERED** OF..

© 1962 by The Chicago Tribune.

..AN' AH'M THE ONLY MAN IN THE WORLD HE'S **LOOKIN'** FOR.

12-1

HIPSHOT'S IN TOWN, REP..HE SENT WORD HE'LL MEET YOU IN THE STREET AT SUNDOWN.

AH'LL BE THERE, MARSHAL.

SO THE GUNFIGHT IS SET FOR **SUNDOWN**, IS IT? **SPLENDID**! I'M BETTING EVEN MONEY ON **HIPSHOT**.

ONLY **YOU** WOULD **BET** ON A SHOOT-OUT, DEUCES..

..BUT **THIS** TIME YOU MIGHT BE SORRY.. 'SPECIALLY. IF YOU'RE BETTIN' HIPSHOT TO **WIN**..

© 1962 by The Chicago Tribune.

..I GOT A **FEELIN'** HE'S ONLY GONNA **PLACE**.

STAN LYNDE

12-3

THE AFTERNOON SUN SINKS LOWER IN THE SKY OVER CONNIPTION..MOVING EVER CLOSER TO **SUNDOWN**.

AFE

OK

© 1962 by The Chicago Tribune.

IN THE CRYSTAL PISTOL SALOON, OLD REP WAITS GRIMLY FOR THE APPOINTED HOUR..

WHILE OVER AT THE HOTEL, HIPSHOT ALSO WAITS, A CONFIDENT SMILE ON HIS FACE..

STAN LYNDE

THAT'S A CONFIDENT SMILE?

DID YOU ALLUS SEND HIPSHOT T' BED WITHOUT HIS SUPPER WHEN HE WAS A YOUNG'UN ?

NO, MARSHAL .. ONLY WHEN HE'D BEEN NAUGHTY.

12-13

HIS MA (BLESS HER) ALLUS USED T' SNEAK HIS SUPPER IN TO HIM .. LATER ON.

WONDERFUL WOMAN, DELLA .. RECKON SHE'D DO IT NOW .. IF'N SHE WAS HERE.

STAN LYNDE

© 1962 by The Chicago Tribune.

ER .. AH'LL HAVE THE BLUE PLATE SPECIAL .. T' GO OUT.

MIDLAND FEEDS

12-14

I THINK IT'S JUST WONDERFUL, RICK .. HIPSHOT AND HIS FATHER REUNITED .. AFTER ALL THESE YEARS.

YEP .. GIVES A FELLER A WARM FEELIN' JUST WATCHIN' 'EM.

I RECKON THERE'S NOTHIN' QUITE AS FINE AS KINFOLKS .. PEOPLE GETTIN' MARRIED, BRINGIN' UP YOUNG'UNS ..

THERE'S SOMETHIN' SORTER SOLID ABOUT MARRIED LIFE .. FOLKS LIVIN' AN' WORKIN' TOGETHER.

VERY TRUE. ER .. HAVEN'T YOU EVER CONSIDERED MARRIAGE, RICK ?

STAN LYNDE

© 1962 by The Chicago Tribune.

ME? SHUCKS, GAYE .. MARRIAGE IS FOR MARRIED MEN .. I'M A BACHELOR !

12-15

AH JES' STOPPED BY T' SAY SO LONG, MARSHAL .. RECKON AH'LL BE MOVIN' ON.

SO SOON ? CAN'T YOU STAY AWHILE, REP ?

WANTED FOR RUSTLING 'Cattle Kate' WRIGHT REWARD

© 1962 by The Chicago Tribune.

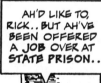

AH'D LIKE TO, RICK .. BUT AH'VE BEEN OFFERED A JOB OVER AT STATE PRISON ..

.. THE WARDEN WANTS ME T' BE HIS ASSISTANT AN' AH'VE DECIDED AH WILL.

STAN LYNDE

AFTER DOIN' SEVEN YEARS ON THE ROCK PILE, PRISON WORK IS WHAT AH KNOW BEST !

159

Current Stan Lynde Titles

Rick O'Shay, Hipshot and Me, A Memoir by Stan Lynde....BK-02

Rick O'Shay and Hipshot, Book 1: The Price of Fame....BK-52

Rick O'Shay and Hipshot, Book 2: The Price of Fame....BK-53

A Month of Sundays, the Best of Rick O'Shay....BK-60

Rick O'Shay, The Dailies: 1959-1960....BK-61

Rick O'Shay, The Dailies: 1961-1962...BK-62

Pardners, Book 1: The Bonding....BK-03

Pardners, Book 2: The Legacy....BK-04

Latigo, Book 1: 1979-1980....BK-20

Latigo, Book 2: 1980-1981....BK-21

Latigo, Book 3: 1981-1983....BK-22

Grass Roots....BK-51

Available through your book dealer or from:

Cottonwood Publishisng, Inc.
2340 Trumble Creek Road
Kalispell, Montana 59901-6713

(address *likely* to change but *phone* # will remain constant)

Cottonwood Clarion Newsletter or Product Catalog

1-800-937-6343